UNDERSTANDING TH

The 'rule of law' is increasingly regarded as integral to liberal democracy, and its significance is frequently discussed by lawyers, academics, politicians and the media. But the meaning of the phrase is not always clear. What does 'the rule of law' mean exactly? And why is it so important to the democratic state and, above all, its citizens?

In *Understanding the Rule of Law*, former President of the Dutch Supreme Court Geert Corstens paints a lively and accessible portrait of the rule of law in practice. The focus is on the role of the courts, where the tensions in a democratic state governed by the rule of law are often discussed and resolved. Using landmark judgments, Geert Corstens explains what judges do and why their work is valuable. What do minimum sentences and prisoners' voting rights have to do with each other? Why is there no easy answer to the question of whether a paedophile organisation should be banned? Why is it no joke when the Italian politician Silvio Berlusconi calls the judiciary 'the cancer of democracy'? *Understanding the Rule of Law* provides the answers to these and many other questions, and is essential reading for anyone interested in the state of democracy today.

Understanding the Rule of Law

Geert Corstens

Translated by Annette Mills from the original Dutch
(*De rechtsstaat moet je leren, de president van de Hoge Raad over de rol
van de rechter*, Prometheus, Amsterdam 2014)

·HART·
PUBLISHING
OXFORD AND PORTLAND, OREGON
2017

Hart Publishing

An imprint of Bloomsbury Publishing Plc

Hart Publishing Ltd
Kemp House
Chawley Park
Cumnor Hill
Oxford OX2 9PH
UK

Bloomsbury Publishing Plc
50 Bedford Square
London
WC1B 3DP
UK

www.hartpub.co.uk
www.bloomsbury.com

Published in North America (US and Canada) by
Hart Publishing
c/o International Specialized Book Services
920 NE 58th Avenue, Suite 300
Portland, OR 97213-3786
USA

www.isbs.com

HART PUBLISHING, the Hart/Stag logo, BLOOMSBURY and the
Diana logo are trademarks of Bloomsbury Publishing Plc

First published 2017

British Library Cataloguing-in-Publication Data

A catalogue record for this book is available from the British Library.

ISBN: HB: 978-1-50990-363-4
        ePDF: 978-1-50990-365-8
        ePub: 978-1-50990-364-1

Library of Congress Cataloging-in-Publication Data

Names: Corstens, G. J. M., author. | Mills, Annette (Translator)

Title: Understanding the rule of law / Geert Corstens ; translated from the original Dutch by Annette Mills.

Other titles: Rechtsstaat moet je leren, de president van de Hoge Raad over de rol van de rechter. English

Description: Oxford [UK] ; Portland, Oregon : Hart Publishing, 2017. |
Includes bibliographical references and index.

Identifiers: LCCN 2017016454 (print) | LCCN 2017017621 (ebook) |
ISBN 9781509903641 (Epub) | ISBN 9781509903634 (pbk. : alk. paper)

Subjects: LCSH: Rule of law. | Rule of law—Netherlands. | Netherlands. Hoge Raad.

Classification: LCC K3171 (ebook) | LCC K3171 .C6713 2017 (print) | DDC 340/.11—dc23

LC record available at https://lccn.loc.gov/2017016454

Typeset by Compuscript Ltd, Shannon
Printed and bound in Great Britain by CPI Group (UK) Ltd, Croydon CR0 4YY

To find out more about our authors and books visit www.hartpublishing.co.uk. Here you will find extracts,
author information, details of forthcoming events and the option to sign up for our newsletters.

MOTTO

'You only know what you're missing when she's gone.'
('Als ze er niet is', De Dijk, 1994)

Foreword

[L]et man learn liberty

From crashing wind and lashing sea.

That chainless wave and lovely land freedom and nationhood demand;[1]

The enduring freedom of the sea to ebb and flow, the freedom of its waves to leap or move in a slumberous roll are guaranteed by the immutable laws of nature. Not surprising, therefore, that the 'chainless wave' would inspire the aspirations of an Irish patriot for liberty and freedom of his own people. This, of course, is an aspiration which is timeless and universal.

We, you and I, may consider ourselves fortunate to live in a modern democratic society which, in spite of its imperfections, guarantees our personal freedoms and fundamental human rights so that we, our families, our friends and those around them have the freedom to choose our path in life and achieve fulfilment as human persons without being restrained by the chains of a dictator or an arbitrary or overbearing government at national or local level. The immutable laws of the universe guarantee such things as the coming and going of seasons and the ebb and flow of the ocean tide. Without these fundamental laws of nature the universe would have collapsed in chaos. The freedoms which we treasure for ourselves and for our communities can only be protected and perhaps more importantly, be maintained if they too are guaranteed by a framework of laws known as the rule of law.

But as the Dane, King Canute, demonstrated to his courtiers in proving that he was powerless to command the incoming sea to stop, the legal framework which guarantees and protects our freedoms is not immutable but merely a manmade construction. One might wish, or more dangerously assume, that the democratic rule of law once established as a framework for a society, will endure without limit or

---

[1] *The West's Awake*, Thomas Davis, 1842–1845.

qualification due to the benign goodwill of those who govern and are governed. Experience and history tell us that this is an assumption that cannot be entertained especially, as Isiah Berlin put it, '*by those who, with Kant, have learned the truth that out of the naked timber of humanity no straight thing was ever made*'.[2] Who would have thought that in the twenty-first century at the highest level of power in the US, torture by interrogators would be considered acceptable, at least when deemed 'useful'. In his own publication on the rule of law, a former senior law lord in the UK, Tom (Lord) Bingham regarded the prohibition on torture as an essential element of the rule of law because '... *there are some practices so abhorrent as not to be tolerable, even when the safety of the State is said to be at risk, ... There are some things which even the supreme power in the State should not be allowed to do, ever.*'[3]

Fortunately, the rule of law means that the US, like other democratic countries, has its particular form of checks and balances. Any executive action which infringes human rights may be checked in the first instance by Congress and ultimately restrained by independent courts, the final guardian of fundamental rights.

Who would have thought that one of the most popular English daily newspapers would publish across its front page large individual photographs of three senior judges above the emblazoned headline, '*ENEMIES OF THE PEOPLE*'.[4] Their sin? To interpret British law as according certain rights to the UK House of Commons in respect of a government decision to leave the European Union. Whipping up such sentiment is hardly conducive to respect for the rule of law. Fortunately, the Rule of Law meant that the remedy against any such perceived sin was an appeal to the UK Supreme Court which, as it happens, upheld the original decision.

Who would have expected the European Union, by decree, to impose obligations on all Member States to store all communications data concerning the private lives of virtually the entire population of the state, including every communication by every individual, child and adult, by text, email, telephone or the Internet.[5] The data collected by

---

[2] Four Essays on Liberty.
[3] *Rule of Law*, Tom Bingham, Allen Laine, 2010, p 17.
[4] *Daily Mail*, 4 November 2016.
[5] Directive 2006/24/EC.

this form of indiscriminate mass surveillance was described by the European Court of Justice, even though the data did not include the content, as data which allowed:

> very precise conclusions to be drawn concerning the private lives of the persons whose data has been retained, such as everyday habits, permanent or temporary places of residence, daily or other movements, the activities carried out, the social relationships of those persons and the social environment frequented by them … In particular, that data provides the means … of establishing a profile of the individuals concerned, information that is no less sensitive, having regard to the right of privacy, than the actual content of communications.[6]

In its case law, the Court of Justice had to strike a balance between the need of a state to combat serious crime and terrorism and what it found to be a serious interference by such a system of data retention with fundamental rights such as the right to privacy and freedom of expression. In striking down the EU Directive and subsequently effectively condemning national legislation which implemented it, the Court, in upholding the rule of law, held that any form of mass data retention must be subject to limitations and to safeguards concerning access to such data in order to ensure that any interference with rights is proportionate to the objective to be achieved.[7]

So we need to warn ourselves that the values and freedoms embodied in a notion such as the rule of law do not survive simply due to the fact that they exist. They will only endure, like pretty well anything else, if we look after them. We will only look after them if we value them. We will only value them if we understand what the rule of law means and the purpose it serves.

But, what is the rule of law? Is it really that important? If so, how does it work, who pulls the levers of power that can affect our rights to a private life, to freedom of expression, the right to education, to health care, or those which protect our environment or consumer rights? How are you and I guaranteed equality of treatment irrespective of gender, colour, religion, sexual orientation or nationality? Are there protections and in particular remedies if somebody rides roughshod over our

---

[6] *Tele2* C-203/15, para 99, 21 December 2016.
[7] See *Digital Rights Ireland C-293/12* and *Tele2 C-203/15*.

rights, even if ostensibly in the name of an apparently laudable objective. This book seeks, successfully in my view, to answer these and the many related questions.

One of the book's many attributes is that, although written by a former judge,[8] it is not addressed to lawyers. It is not a textbook. It is addressed to those who probably have a fair idea that a thing called the rule of law is probably good for the stability of society and the protection of our freedoms but is not sure how it works, or rather how it must work, and who may not be fully aware how easily the protection of rights is susceptible to being undermined by state action. Another attribute of the book that it is replete with day to day interesting examples and explanation of the rule of law in action including the interaction between the primary organs of government, the Executive, the Legislators and the Judiciary. Although many of the examples given stem from experiences of the Dutch legal system, any reader can readily identify with those experiences as ones which parallel everyday experiences in any country whose system claims to be founded on the rule of law. The relaxed narrative style of the author also helps make the book a good read.

I have been fortunate because of my vocation, to have a long experience at comparing legal systems and in particular experiencing the diversity in constitutional structures between different countries. As a judge, for eight years, at the Court of Justice of the European Union, one could readily discern that the differences between countries and their legal systems were indeed essentially structural and procedural. But what is equally clear is that all constitutional frameworks in the modern liberal democracy, whatever their structure, are founded on the same fundamental values concerning the rights of the individual and equality before the law. The rule of law is a common golden thread in the fabric of every liberal democracy. In short, this is an informative book for all citizens in any democratic country.

One of the fundamental reasons why this book is important is that it imparts knowledge on a subject too frequently left to experts. Far too often have I seen various actors in society, politicians or the media for example, invoke and pay lip service to the 'Rule of Law'. It often

---

[8] Former President of the Supreme Court of the Netherlands.

becomes apparent that they do not have much of an understanding of what this means or the duties which it imposes on them to respect the rights of others, including minorities, and the institutions of the state, such as the courts, who are tasked with vindicating and protecting such rights. I would hope that lots of politicians would read this book but more important, that the non-lawyer citizen does so. The law and the administration of justice belong to the people, not to law-makers, lawyers or judges. The greater the spread of knowledge and understanding of the rule of law, particularly when a resurgent populism can drive leaders to overlook or override basic rights, the more readily can those who govern be called to account by its citizens.

I share with the author an attachment to the words of Pericles which he quotes—'*[o]ur Constitution is called a democracy because the power is in the hands not of a minority but of the whole people.*' I have previously commented on this when I wrote:

> This sentiment is as valid today as it was when expressed by Pericles in his funeral oration, honouring the dead soldiers of the Peloponnesian War in 430 B.C. It was evident in the post-Homeric age, when the first hazy conceptual embryos of formal law emerged. The democratic sentiment was present in the ensuing era of the Hellenic world when the first efforts were made to inscribe in permanent and public form rules which formerly had the more insubstantial status of custom. That is the spring from which the idea of the rule of law in organised society emerged, spread to the Roman world from where it flowed inexorably over the centuries across Europe; and eventually to the New World so that the idea of law, although in a constant state of evolution, is today the lifeblood of the modern democratic state.[9]

Laws protecting democratic values and freedoms have a clear purpose, as Justice Robert Jackson of the US Supreme Court pointed out in the seminal case of *West Virginia Board of Education v Barnette*:[10]

> The very purpose of a Bill of Rights was to withdraw certain subjects from the vicissitudes of political controversy, to place them beyond the reach of majorities [or functionaries] and to establish them as legal principles to be applied by the courts. One's right to life, liberty and property, to free speech, a free press, freedom of worship and assembly, and other fundamental rights may not be submitted to vote; they depend on the outcome of no elections.

[9] New England Law Review Vol. 41, no 2.
[10] 319 US 624(943).

This book is a document which explains in a fascinating and often entertaining manner, what the Rule of Law really is, how it works, the role played by an independent judiciary and why it is so important for the very purpose identified by Justice Jackson.

John Murray
Former president of the Supreme Court of Ireland,
former member of the Court of Justice of the European Union
January 2017

Acknowledgements

My thanks go to appellate judge Reindert Kuiper, who contributed enormously to the Dutch version of this book; to John Spencer, Professor of Law at Cambridge University, who answered my numerous enquiries about English law; and to Madeleine Corstens-Mignot who—once again—inspired me and was unfailingly patient.

Contents

Introduction

Perhaps you saw the highly criticised headlines in the *Daily Mail* of 4 November 2016 below pictures of three High Court judges: 'Enemies of the people' and 'Fury over "out of touch" judges who defied 17.4 m Brexit voters and could trigger constitutional crisis'. While in the Netherlands, people might have seen on TV or in the newspapers headlines such as: 'Female SGP member elected to local council' and 'Netherlands held responsible in Srebrenica case'. The SGP headline referred to the Dutch Calvinist Party, an orthodox Protestant political party that until 2006 opposed party membership for women; the Srebrenica case involved proceedings brought by relatives of the Bosnian Muslims who died while under the protection of Dutch UN forces.

Just three news items among many. And you could simply read over them, unless you knew the background. They appear to speak for themselves, but in fact are the result of the highly developed state of the rule of law in the western world today. The judgment of the High Court could not have been rendered if there was no concept of the separation of powers. And the many complaints about this headline could not have been made if there was no idea about the importance of the independence of judges. The item on the SGP council member could not have been written if there was no international community within which the UN Convention on the Elimination of All Forms of Discrimination Against Women could be drawn up and if there was no legislature to ratify that convention. Nor would it have appeared if the Netherlands had no constitution allowing the courts to assess national laws in light of international treaties. Last but not least, without the efforts of the 'Mothers of Srebrenica' foundation, the case would never have been brought. And would the ruling ever have come about without a proper legal aid system and an independent judiciary? Or if we had what they called 'telephone justice' in the former Soviet Union, where at some point judges would receive a phone call from one of the party bosses, who would issue instructions on how to rule in a particular case?

In this book I try to explain the significance of the rule of law and the role of the judiciary in a democratic state governed by the rule of law. Not by taking theory as my starting point, but by looking at the players involved, providing an insight through a variety of specific cases into what they (and in particular the judges) do, why they do it and why their actions are important and valuable. Weighty tomes in complex language can and have been written about the institutions of a state governed by the rule of law. My aim here is to do the opposite, to paint using concrete examples a lively picture of how the judiciary operates and its relationship with the other branches of government. The topics are wide-ranging: for example, why are Montesquieu's ideas about the separation of powers still so relevant? What do minimum sentences, Ayaan Hirsi Ali (a Somali-born Dutch-American activist, author and politician) and Srebrenica have to do with each other? Why is it difficult to decide whether a paedophile association should be banned? Why was it so important that US president Eisenhower sent troops to Little Rock in order to implement a judgment of the US Supreme Court? Why is it no laughing matter when Silvio Berlusconi describes the judiciary as the 'cancer of democracy'? Why is it so significant that after the Supreme Court had ruled against the State the Dutch Prime Minister Mark Rutte remarked 'It goes without saying that the court's decision will now be implemented'? This book aims to provide the answers to these and many other questions.

But why would you, the reader, be interested in this? 'Knowledge about our government is not handed down by the gene pool, it has to be learned,' says Sandra Day O'Connor, the first woman to serve on the US Supreme Court. Research shows that two-thirds of Americans can name a member of the *American Idol* jury, but only 15% know the name of the Chief Justice of the US Supreme Court. No more than a third of the population can name the three branches of government. In the absence of comparable research, dare we hope that things are different in European countries? In any event, shedding some light on the work judges do in states governed by the rule of law can only be a good thing, it seems to me. In doing so, I follow in the footsteps of Sandra Day O'Connor, who once said 'an old judge is like an old shoe—everything is all worn out except the tongue'.

1

A Democratic State Governed by the Rule of Law: What Does This Mean?

'EVERY BANANA REPUBLIC has a bill of rights' said the late Justice Antonin Scalia in 2011. He went on to explain that without the separation of powers, such a document had nevertheless no meaning: it was just 'words on paper'.

> The bill of rights of the former evil empire, the Union of Soviet Socialist Republics, was much better than ours. I mean it literally. [But] the constitution of the Soviet Union did not prevent the centralisation of power in one person or in one party. And when that happens the game is over.

Scalia and Justice Stephen Breyer, both members of the US Supreme Court, were testifying before a public hearing of the US Senate Judiciary Committee on the role of judges under the US Constitution.

Scalia went on to say that only when there is a sound government structure, including an independent judiciary, do those 'words on paper' acquire practical meaning and are rights enforceable.

Take a look at Turkey, for example. In March 2014 the media reported that Prime Minister Recep Tayyip Erdoğan (now President) had blocked the use of Twitter. A newspaper report claimed that he was angry because recordings of conversations in which he allegedly instructed his son to remove large amounts of cash from a private residence in connection with a police corruption probe had been posted on Twitter. He demanded that the offending links be removed. When Twitter failed to do so, access to the site was blocked. Erdoğan claimed that the recordings were fabricated, as part of a plot to blacken the governing party's name in the run-up to the local government elections on 30 March.

A week later Turkey blocked YouTube as well. On 2 April 2014, the Turkish Constitutional Court ruled that the Twitter ban had to be lifted because it violated freedom of expression, guaranteed by the Turkish constitution.[1] By that time, the Turkish local elections were over. So this was hardly a resounding victory for free speech. And yet, a democratically elected government could not just do what it wanted. It too was bound by the law. That is the essence of a democratic state governed by the rule of law.

The term 'democratic state under the rule of law' means a state where citizens elect their own leaders, a state where government itself is bound by the law and helps ensure that the law is respected in the relations between citizens. The law guarantees everyone's individual freedoms against contraventions by government or other citizens. This can only happen if the legislature, executive and judiciary are separate. And a crucial element is an independent court system which is truly accessible to the citizen. On paper, such a state could be established overnight, as it were, given the knowledge, experience and the models available to us nowadays. But in practice, even today the rule of law requires decades to grow and become meaningful. That is also true in the western world.

People in the western world live in democratic states under the rule of law. A simple but significant example follows: the Dutch state took its argument that it was not responsible for the deaths of three Muslims who had been sent away from the UN compound manned by Dutch peacekeeping forces in Bosnia right up to the highest court. But when this court finally decided otherwise, the Prime Minister said 'We will of course act in accordance with this ruling. That is what happens in a state governed by the rule of law'.

This seems very straightforward but it isn't. The rule of law in the Netherlands too has evolved step-by-step.

I. FROM LITTLE ROCK TO HUNGARY

The rule of law does not come about automatically, and without constant effort and maintenance it cannot continue to exist. Stephen Breyer, associate justice of the US Supreme Court, once gave the

---

[1] It would be interesting if the Turkish court were to explain its ruling in a YouTube clip and post a link to the judgment on Twitter, as the Dutch Supreme Court often does.

example of a chief justice in an African country who asked him: 'Why do Americans do what the courts say?' She wondered what the secret was.

Breyer answered that there was no secret, that 'following the law is a matter of custom, of habit, of widely shared understandings as to how those in government and members of the public should [...] act when faced with a court decision they strongly dislike. That habit and widely shared understanding cannot be achieved without a struggle; it is a long, gradual development based on experience'.[2]

In the US too, the rule of law did not come about without a struggle. In 1954, in the case of *Brown v Board of Education*, the US Supreme Court prohibited the racial segregation in public education that had existed till then in the southern states. From then on, black students had to be admitted to the hitherto white Central High School in Little Rock, Arkansas. Led by Governor Orval Faubus, Arkansas opposed this development and defied the Supreme Court ruling. President Eisenhower understood that there would be little left of the rule of law if state governments could henceforth decide themselves which judgments they would abide by and which not. He announced on television that he was sending federal troops to Arkansas. He sent the 101st Airborne Division, revered by Americans as heroes of the Second World War. On 24 September 1957, 52 aircraft with 1,000 soldiers on board flew to Little Rock. They protected the first nine black pupils registered at the school from an angry white crowd at the school gates. Ultimately, their actions ensured that the nine pupils could continue to attend Central High. It is not difficult to imagine the situation that would arise if the decisions of the courts were ignored. In essence, we would return to the law of the jungle.

The same applies if the judiciary is not independent. The 'evil empire' Scalia referred to, Ronald Reagan's description of the former Soviet Union, did have a court system but it was characterised by what was known as 'telephone justice'. This has nothing to do with the modern custom of hearing witnesses in court cases by video link to save them long journeys. Telephone justice means that the judge receives a phone call from a party boss who instructs him on how to rule in a particular case.

---

[2] See S Breyer, *Making Our Democracy Work, a Judge's View*, New York, Alfred A Knopf, 2011, pp 22–23.

II. THE VULNERABILITY OF THE RULE OF LAW

Creating a democracy under the rule of law—where the law is more than flimsy 'words on paper', where government action is genuinely bound by the rules of law and where citizens have genuine access to the courts—demands time, integrity and constant commitment. Not only from the judiciary, but also from the other two branches of government, the executive and the legislature. All three must constantly articulate the message of the rule of law. This is necessary because the viability and the quality of the rule of law ultimately depends for the most part on the people. If they elect leaders who cut off access to the courts, or want to abolish the review of legislation in light of human rights treaties, the rule of law could decline rapidly. The rule of law in a democracy is not self-evident. It is not a binary concept, one or zero, a case of all or nothing. Instead, the rule of law exists in various degrees of quality. And once high quality is achieved it does not continue to exist without support.

Knowledge of the significance of the rule of law and a commitment to its cause must be passed on from generation to generation if it is to survive. 'Liberty,' wrote the eminent US judge Billings Learned Hand, 'lies in the hearts of men and women; when it dies there, no constitution, no law, no court can save it; no constitution, no law, no court can even do much to help it.'[3]

The same applies to modern Europe. Yet quite recently the Polish Government undermined the position of the Polish Constitutional Tribunal by ignoring some of their rulings. Some authors have spoken of a 'creeping assault on the Constitution'.[4] The European Commission's first vice-president Frans Timmermans tried to convince the Polish that the measures taken by the Polish Government and parliament ran counter to the rule of law as referred to in article 2 of the Treaty on European Union:

> The Union is founded on the values of respect for human dignity, freedom, democracy, equality, the rule of law and respect for human rights, including

---

[3] Billings Learned Hand, *The Spirit of Liberty*, published in 1952.

[4] Dariusz Mazur and Waldemar Żurek, 'First year of the so-called "Good change" in the Polish system of the administration of justice', December 2016 issue of *Státní zastupitelství* (Public Prosecutor), the journal of Czech public prosecutors: www.nsz.cz/index.php/en/magazine-public-prosecution.

the rights of persons belonging to minorities. These values are common to the Member States in a society in which pluralism, non-discrimination, tolerance, justice, solidarity and equality between women and men prevail.

To date, these efforts have not resulted in major changes guaranteeing the proper functioning of the Constitutional Tribunal.

Similarly, and not so very long ago, in EU Member State Hungary, Viktor Orbán's democratically elected government lowered the retirement age for judges by eight years. This happened at a time when the country was enormously in debt and, in the European context, people were being encouraged to work longer to keep pensions affordable. At the same time measures were taken that greatly increased the ruling party's influence on the appointments of new judges to fill the hundreds of vacancies that arose. What is more, the highest Hungarian judge, Chief Justice András Baka (who had also been elected as President of the Network of the Presidents of the Supreme Judicial Courts of the EU) was removed from his post before the expiry of his mandate. The reason given was that according to yet another new rule he did not have the required five years' experience in the national judicial system, despite the fact that he had 17 years' experience as a judge in the European Court of Human Rights (ECtHR). Baka had in fact opposed a number of the Government's plans.[5] The measures were reminiscent of those taken in the Netherlands by the German occupiers at the beginning of the war. There too the retirement age for judges was reduced, while the President of the Supreme Court was dismissed because he was Jewish. In both situations this created room to appoint judges sympathetic to the regime.

The European Commission tried to call Hungary to heel, the European Court of Justice found the sudden reduction in the retirement age to be in breach of European law[6] and the European Court of Human Rights ruled that the removal of Baka was incompatible with the European Convention on Human Rights (ECHR).[7]

Yet none of this seemed to affect Orbán's popularity at the time. In the elections held in the spring of 2014, his party obtained for a second time a two-thirds majority in the Hungarian parliament. At the end of July, Orbán said they were building an illiberal or non-liberal state like

---

[5] ECtHR, 27 May 2014, 20261/12 (*Baka v Hungary*).
[6] ECJ, 2 November 2012, C-286/12 (*European Commission v Hungary*).
[7] ECtHR, 27 May 2014, 20261/12 (*European Commission v Hungary*).

that in China or Russia, claiming that the financial crisis had shown that liberal democracies would not be able to 'sustain their world-competitiveness' in the years ahead. Hungary and Poland remind us of the vulnerability of the existing system, hammering home the message that whether the rule of law flourishes or fails is determined through democratic channels.

Since the end of the Second World War, the state of the rule of law has, on the whole, improved in most European countries. Slowly but surely safeguards to protect its survival are being constructed. This does not mean that relapse isn't possible, as has happened in Hungary and Poland. But in such cases direct mechanisms generally come into effect to restore the rule of law.

In all 47 of the Council of Europe (CoE) Member States, governments nowadays are held to account if they fail to take sufficient account of fundamental rights. But this is not an automatic process. We have to fight for it. Think for example of developments in Russia, where homosexuality is still regarded as wrong and unnatural. In this battle minorities no longer stand alone, precisely because of the European Convention and its enforcement mechanisms. They know that they have right on their side. And that is a great achievement, from a legal and a moral perspective.

Article 7 of the Treaty on European Union provides for a mechanism to determine that there is a clear risk of a serious breach by a Member State of the values referred to in article 2 and to sanction this Member State. Sometimes this is called 'the nuclear option'. In 2014 the European Commission established a 'framework to safeguard the rule of law in the European Union'. This new framework included an early warning tool allowing the Commission to enter into a dialogue with the Member State concerned to prevent the escalation of systemic threats to the rule of law. In cases where no solution is found within the new EU rule of law framework, article 7 will always remain the last resort to resolve a crisis and ensure compliance with European Union values. The rule of law framework is now being applied with regard to Poland.

III. DEMOCRACY FROM PERICLES TO HITLER'S GERMANY

Our constitution does not copy the laws of neighbouring states; we are rather a pattern to others than imitators ourselves. Its administration favours the many instead of the few; this is why it is called a democracy. If we look to the laws, they afford equal justice to all in their private differences; if no social standing, advancement in public life falls to reputation for capacity; class considerations not being allowed to interfere with merit; nor again does poverty bar the way, if a man is able to serve the state, he is not hindered by the obscurity of his condition.[8]

These words come from an oration given by the Greek statesman Pericles (495–429 BCE), at a funeral ceremony for the fallen at the end of the first year of the Peloponnesian war.

Literally, democracy means government by the people. It is a venerable concept that relies on the principle that all human beings are equal. People enter into a contract with each other and are prepared to subject themselves to its rules as long as they are allowed in one way or another to participate in deciding the terms of that contract. Of course, equal rights in fact only applied to male citizens in ancient Greece, but it was a start.

The idea that people in society enter into a contract with others is of course theoretical. After all it is difficult to ask each and every person after they have been born whether they wish to subscribe to this contract and if they do, under what conditions. We are all part of a history that cannot be erased. The only meaningful solution to this problem is to enable people to choose the way their state and society is generally organised through their representatives. This is modern representative democracy as it exists in many countries. It is simply not possible to allow everyone to discuss everything. Often decisions have to be taken rapidly. You cannot wait until a disaster takes place.

Where less urgent but nonetheless significant decisions are concerned, the idea of a referendum is sometimes mooted: the entire electorate is consulted about a specific plan. This is what took place on 18 September 2014 in Scotland: every person who was entitled to vote could state whether they were for or against independence for their country. The traditional objection to the referendum is that a single question is put to the people without reference to its connection with other issues. For example, if you were to ask the electorate if income tax should be reduced by 10%, you would run the risk that euphoria about lower taxes might blind people to the fact that this would lead to cuts in public services.

---

[8] From a translation by Richard Crawley of Thucydides' *The History of the Peloponnesian War.*

In a representative democracy where the broad organisation of state and society is established by the representatives of the people, it is usually possible to arrive at feasible solutions which have the approval of the majority of the representatives. In the best possible scenario that majority corresponds to a majority of the electorate. In the worst possible scenario, there is a large gap between the two.

Nowadays, democracy is based much more on the equality of all human beings (not just male citizens), in contrast to Pericles' time. And it means that everyone must be able to express his or her views. A two-tier society, like that of the Greeks and later in the era of slavery, or of racial segregation as in the US and South Africa, is therefore unacceptable. The right to vote must not be based on wealth or income, or on gender. In a modern democracy, the right to vote is universal.

Time and again, democracy and the rule of law are mentioned in the same breath. In this book, I do it too. But they are not synonymous. A democracy is not automatically a state governed by the rule of law. In 1930s Germany, Hitler's dictatorship came into being through democratic decision-making.[9] Under his leadership the Nuremburg race laws were enacted in 1935. These were founded on the idea that people were not equal: they discriminated against Jews. The South African apartheid system too was based on human inequality. What is more, the 'marketing' of segregation in the US, under the motto 'Separate but equal' could not hide the fact that black people were systematically discriminated against. Discrimination based on characteristics like race, origin or religion is regarded as incompatible with human dignity and therefore with the principles of the rule of law. Human dignity means

---

[9] 'Adolf Hitler (1889–1945) became Chancellor of Germany on 30 January 1933. On 27 February 1933, an arson attack was carried out on the *Reichstag* (German parliament building) for which the Dutch national Marinus van der Lubbe (1909–1934) was convicted and sentenced to death by beheading on 10 January 1934 in Leipzig. In the elections following the fire, held on 5 March 1933, the Nazi Party (NSDAP) made substantial gains but did not obtain an absolute majority. A few weeks later, on 22 March 1933, the new regime opened the first concentration camp in Dachau. One day later, Hitler and his adherents persuaded parliament to proclaim the Enabling Act (*Ermächtigungsgesetz*) which together with the Reichstag Fire Decree (*Reichstagsbrandverordnung*) granted the new government dominated by the National Socialists far-reaching powers which were not subject to parliamentary scrutiny. Hitler's dictatorship was born.' From *De Hoge Raad en de Tweede Wereldoorlog* (The Dutch Supreme Court and the Second World War) by Corjo Jansen and Derk Venema, Amsterdam, Boom, 2011, p 5.

that nobody is judged on the basis of his or her gender, descent, ethnicity, sexual orientation, political affiliation, religion, philosophy of life, etc. All these characteristics determine his or her individuality and must be accepted. People should be judged on their actions.

What I'm trying to say is that it is possible for legislation that is flagrantly in breach of the concept of the rule of law to be passed through democratic processes. On the other hand, it is barely conceivable for the rule of law to exist without democracy. After all, as we saw just now, the idea of the rule of law is based on equality among citizens. In that case how could one defend a form of government like a dictatorship or an oligarchy? Of course, you could theoretically elect a dictator through democratic processes and guarantee that in due course he would be set aside through those same processes. And there are republics that grant a great deal of power to their presidents, like the US and—to a lesser degree—France and, presumably in the near future, Turkey. Monarchies are another variation on this theme. In Europe at least, monarchs have few powers and it is possible to change the constitution in order to abolish the monarchy. There is thus no dictatorship by the sovereign, just as in the modern Western republics referred to just now there is no dictatorship of the president. What is more, in those modern democracies both sovereigns and presidents are bound by the law.

Dictatorship only exists when there are no checks on the 'leader' and there is no representative assembly standing in his way. Where this happens, it is not only morally wrong; it is not viable in the long term. European and South American history has demonstrated this time and again. The Arab Spring would seem to confirm it. There too, people demanded an end to repressive regimes, more political freedom, democracy and human rights. They wanted an end to corruption, unemployment and food shortages. We know of no better model than a democracy under the rule of law to achieve those aims. Because if it is stable, such a state also offers the best economic environment. The World Justice Project's Rule of Law Index shows that the quality of the rule of law in a country runs in tandem with its gross national product. Countries where the rule of law is weak also score less well in terms of prosperity; the converse is also true.[10] The explanation is fairly

---

[10] The World Justice Project is supported by the Neukom Family Foundation and the Bill and Melinda Gates Foundation.

simple: no one wants to do business with or in a country where agreements cannot be enforced and the only thing that ultimately counts is the opinion of a ruler who is not subject to checks and balances. Justice Breyer's remarks on this subject are well worth considering. He believes that companies will not want to invest in countries where the rule of law is not respected, where government is corrupt, where if you become involved in a dispute you are unable to gain access to an independent and impartial tribunal, where there is no predictability whatsoever. Breyer in turn quoted Alan Greenspan's observation that 'the rule of law and property rights appear to me to be the most prominent institutional pillars of economic growth and prosperity'.[11]

IV. THE RULE OF LAW AND THE MALTREATMENT OF PENGUINS

L'état, c'est moi. ('I am the state').

Every man's house is his castle. Even though the winds of heaven may blow through it, the King of England may not enter it.[12]

In other words, in his own home even the poorest man can resist the power of the monarch.

So if you maltreat a penguin in the London zoo, you do not escape prosecution because you are the Archbishop of Canterbury.[13]

The first quotation is attributed to King Louis XIV, known as the Sun King and an absolute monarch. He believed himself to be above the law. The second quotation expresses the opposite view: even the King is bound by the law. And the third says the same thing in a different way: however lofty your position, you have to observe the law. No one is above the law, not the king or his ministers or the highest judges.

---

[11] Alan Greenspan, *The Age of Turbulence: Adventures in a New World*, Penguin Books, New York 2007, p 255.

[12] Likely source is William Pitt, Earl of Chatham, in a speech before the House of Commons in 1766. See B H Rosenwein, *Negotiating Space, Power, Restraint and Privileges of Immunity in Early Mediaeval Europe*, Manchester University Press, 1999, p 184.

[13] T Bingham, *The Rule of Law*, London, Allan Lane, 2010, p 4.

How is it possible that the King himself may not enter your house without your permission, today as in the past? The reason is that the inviolability of the home is enshrined and protected in various constitutions and the European Convention on Human Rights. Any exceptions must be clearly defined in law. Consequently, sound legislation is required to ensure that basic rights cannot be too easily infringed. That is the task of the legislature. The executive, including the police, has to obey those laws. But if there are no checks on compliance with the law it is possible for its practical significance to decline; it becomes simply 'words on paper'. In this sense, the judiciary plays an important role. It keeps the executive in check.

The law governs the relations between citizens and between citizens and government. The words attributed to Louis XIV are thus in line with his vision of himself as God's representative on earth, but they are completely incompatible with the rule of law. 'Equal justice under law' is engraved on the front of the US Supreme Court building. An idea that would have given the Sun King the cold shivers. He decided himself which rules would apply to him.

In a state governed by the rule of law everyone is equal before the law: high-ranking officials are also bound by the law, including the Archbishop of Canterbury. But sometimes you have to go to court to experience that that is the case.

V. THE SEPARATION OF POWERS: MONTESQUIEU AND BERLUSCONI

Another famous Frenchman, Montesquieu, made an immense contribution towards ensuring that power does not come to rest in a single body, so that no one is above the law. 'C'est une expérience éternelle que tout homme qui a du pouvoir est porté à en abuser (…) Pour qu'on ne puisse abuser du pouvoir, il faut que, par la disposition des choses, le pouvoir arrête le pouvoir.' As one English translation puts it: '[It is] an eternal experiment, and one any man with power is tempted to abuse. […] If power is not to be abused, the world must be so organised that power puts a stop to power'.[14]

---

[14] Translation by Parliament of Canada.

Montesquieu explained the concept of the separation of powers in *De l'esprit des lois* (The Spirit of Laws), published in 1748. The essence of this idea is that legislative, executive and judicial power must not be held by one body or person. These three branches of government must be kept in balance to reduce the chances of an abuse of power. Because different institutions exercise the legislative, executive and judicial powers, each of them can call the others to heel where necessary. In this way they keep one other in check and prevent one branch assuming too much power.

Think, for example, of the former Italian Prime Minister Silvio Berlusconi, who once tried to create immunity under the law for himself to avoid prosecution. The Italian Constitutional Court refused to go along with this and declared the law in question unconstitutional, on the grounds that everyone is equal before the law.

Even today, many elements of the way the state is organised in European countries go back to the ideas of Montesquieu. The various constitutions and the legislation based upon them are imbued with the idea of the separation of powers. This prevents a concentration of power that might give someone the idea that he or she can stand above the law like a Sun King. Under the rule of law, everyone is bound by the law.

The three branches of government—the legislature, the executive and the judiciary—keep each other in check in making and implementing laws. The legislature draws the broad lines which the executive puts into practice. Then the courts decide in the individual cases brought before them. This balance also means that the legislature can adjust legislation following a court decision, after which the courts may be asked to interpret the new law and to apply it within the limits determined by the constitution and international law (if review on these grounds is allowed). This is an ongoing process. In other words, under the rule of law no one has the last word.

VI. PROTECTING HUMAN RIGHTS

Protecting everyone's fundamental rights, otherwise known as human rights, is a crucial aspect of the rule of law. These are rights arising from the dignity of each human being, like the right to life and the right to freedom of expression. They guarantee everyone's individual freedoms, including those of people who belong to an ethnic, religious or other minority.

> Human rights are rights accruing to everyone everywhere in the world. Their purpose is to protect people against the power of the state and must ensure that everyone can retain their human dignity. For example, they mean that every individual can have and express his or her own opinion freely. Or that the government may not use random violence against its citizens. They include the right to education, enough to eat and a roof above your head. States have agreed with each other that they will guarantee these rights for everyone. Regardless of race, colour, sex, language, religion, political or other opinion, national or social background, prosperity, birth or any other status. Human rights form the basis for all legislation and policy laid down by government.

This is how the Netherlands Institute for Human Rights explains the concept on its website.

Human rights are the backbone of our civilisation. They are enshrined in the highest legal sources, like international treaties and constitutions. This confers on them a powerful legal status. For it is not easy to change the constitution or a treaty. Former associate justice of the US Supreme Court, William Brennan, once stated that the purpose of the constitution was to declare that certain rights were of a higher order and to put them 'beyond the reach of temporary political majorities'.[15] That is singularly apt. It also makes it clear why judges who are not directly, democratically elected are entitled to review legislation: because they have to award priority to a higher source of law. Especially when a temporary political majority wishes to do something which is incompatible with those sources or if the executive fails to respect fundamental rights.

In many countries courts may review the constitutionality of legislation and treaties. Individual human rights can also be protected against breaches by the legislature or executive via international human rights treaties. To a large extent, we have the role played by the European Convention on Human Rights (ECHR) in recent decades to thank for this. The Convention was concluded in Rome on 4 November 1950.

---

[15] William J Brennan Jr, 'The Constitution of the United States', in David M. O'Brien (ed.), *Judges on Judging*, Washington D.C., CQ Press, 2009, pp 212–223, p 215. 'It is the very purpose of a Constitution—and particularly of a Bill of Rights—to declare certain values transcendent, beyond the reach of temporary majorities.'

It was preceded by the Universal Declaration of Human Rights adopted by the General Assembly of the United Nations on 10 December 1948. The aim of the Declaration was to prevent as far as possible future injustice and atrocities such as those perpetrated during the Second World War (as a result of events in Nazi Germany). The ECHR establishes an explicit link with the Universal Declaration by referring to the contracting parties as 'likeminded and [with] a common heritage of political traditions, ideals, freedom and the rule of law'. The ECHR also established an international court, the European Court of Human Rights, responsible for monitoring respect for human rights, as enshrined in the Convention, once all national remedies have been exhausted.

VII. BALANCE BETWEEN THE POWERS WITH FREEDOM OF THE CITIZEN AS ITS FUNDAMENT

We have thus a complex interplay of issues: government must be bound by the law, the settlement of disputes and imposition of penalties must be the province of the judiciary, fundamental rights must be respected. The underlying priority is that the freedoms of citizens must be protected. The state organisation is not there to thwart the people, but must aim to promote the freedom and welfare of us all. If the legislature saddles us with laws which substantially limit our freedoms, it is fortunately always possible to have recourse to the courts. They can assess whether such a limitation on freedom was excessive in a specific case. For example, whether it was permissible to make wearing the niqab a criminal offence. Or if granting tax advantages to businesses was overly prejudicial for private persons. If the legislature passes rigorous legislation, the executive can sometimes try to temper its effect when it is implemented.

As we saw earlier, the concept of the rule of law is based on the separation of powers. We accept the exercise of powers by others because rules are necessary to achieve a degree of order in society. And those rules have to be enforced. Traditionally, we have the legislature that sets general rules, the government which applies those rules in its actions and the courts which in the event of disputes between citizens, companies, institutions or government agencies, or of failure by citizens to observe the rules of law, provide a solution or impose penalties.

That is why it is so important for citizens, institutions and companies to have easy access to the courts. It is pointless to grant decision-making powers to an independent and impartial judiciary if it is impossible to have recourse to the courts, because litigation is too expensive, too time-consuming or too complex. In such circumstances the legislative and executive branches can act unchecked. I'll return to this point in subsequent chapters.

In answer to the question of why we have the rule of law, the former head of the Dutch Scientific Council for Government Policy (which published a report in 2002 entitled *The future of the national constitutional state*), Michiel Scheltema, responded that it was 'to protect citizens from arbitrariness and to guarantee legal certainty and equality of treatment'.[16] The rule of law is there for citizens.

If the executive over-extends its powers in a way that affects individual citizens, the legislature can call the executive to heel. It can, for example, prohibit the police from searching people if there are no good grounds for suspecting that they have committed a criminal offence. The courts too can intervene at the request of a citizen whose freedom has been infringed in this way. And if the courts assume too much power, the legislature can call them to heel through new legislation. This is also possible through new international law if a court has based its ruling on international law.

In this way an equilibrium is established. In other words—and I'm going to repeat this several times—no one has the last word, not even political leaders. In this context the phrase 'the primacy of the political sphere' is sometimes heard. This is based on a misconception: that it is politicians who make the ultimate decisions. And that idea is the reverse of how things should work in a democratic state governed by the rule of law: each of the powers holds the other in check, so a balance is achieved. The result is moderation, one of the four cardinal virtues.[17] This is not to say that the legislature must always be circumspect. In a democracy it is the legislature's responsibility to set out the broad structure of the state and—depending on one's political opinions— of society. The legislature also determines the conditions subject to

[16] M Scheltema, *Staatscourant* (Government Gazette), no. 36, 20 February 2003, p 5.

[17] Moderation (*temperantia*), courage (*fortitudo*), wisdom (*prudentia*) and justice (*justitia*) are the four cardinal virtues, derived initially from Plato's scheme.

which government may act against its citizens. Legislation is enacted by the government of the day together with the representatives of the people; it is thus the expression of what they believe to be necessary and desirable. It is also the basis for the decisions taken by the executive and the judiciary. Which means those decisions too are democratically sanctioned. Later, we will see that laws do not regulate matters down to the smallest detail and that they sometimes contain loopholes. Or can be overtaken by new developments the legislator had not anticipated.

Here we have a broad outline of a democracy governed by the rule of law. It may sound very abstract. So perhaps an example of the opposite might be useful. In other words, what does a country look like without the rule of law, a state where no one is bound by the law? In 2012 a Dutch daily newspaper described the situation in the Democratic Republic of the Congo as follows. 'Politicians steal freely from the state. The government pays no salaries, or they "get mislaid", so teachers ask parents for bribes. No policeman will accept a complaint without "motivation money". Journalists pay members of the security services to avoid arrest. Soldiers whose wages have not been paid loot and plunder, while militia members commit rape.'[18]

Under the rule of law, the fact that everyone is bound by the law serves to protect our freedom and our human dignity. Nevertheless, living in society presupposes certain curtailments of that freedom by others and by government. Living in a community requires tolerance and moderation (*temperantia*, in Latin). This involves listening to others, taking account of the interests and values of others, being slow to demonise others. What matters for the rule of law is that only properly legitimised infringements on our freedoms are allowed, and that there is no imbalance between the power held by government and citizens. In a democracy governed by the rule of law power is conferred by the law, not by rulers. The law creates possibilities but also determines their limits.

---

[18]   *NRC Handelsblad*, 17 September 2012.

2

What is the Role of the Judiciary in a Democratic State Governed by the Rule of Law?

The United States is a "government of laws, not of men". Under such a government, "where there is a legal right, there is also a legal remedy". Indeed, "the very essence of civil liberty certainly consists in the right of every individual to claim the protection of the laws, whenever he receives an injury".[1]

IN OTHER WORDS, the essence of fundamental rights—such as freedom of expression, the right to privacy and the right to due process—is that every individual has the right and the opportunity to have recourse to the protection offered by the law against infringements of those freedoms.

I. TAKING JUSTICE INTO ONE'S OWN HANDS, TRIAL BY JURY AND AN INDEPENDENT JUDICIARY

The quotation at the beginning of this chapter echoes *The Federalist Papers*, a collection of articles and essays written by Alexander Hamilton, James Madison and John Jay, published under the pen name 'Publius' between 27 October 1787 and 28 May 1788, the period in which the US Constitution was signed and (partially) ratified. It is interesting to note the similarities with the following texts from the European Convention for the Protection of Human Rights and Fundamental Freedoms (ECHR), which came into effect over 150 years later.

In the determination of his civil rights and obligations or of any criminal charge against him, everyone is entitled to a fair and public hearing within

---

[1] Stephen Breyer 2011, *op. cit.*, p 17 (quoting John Adams, among others).

a reasonable time by an independent and impartial tribunal established by law.[2]

Everyone whose rights and freedoms as set forth in this Convention are violated shall have an effective remedy before a national authority notwithstanding that the violation has been committed by persons acting in an official capacity.[3]

The aim of the Convention is to guarantee that our human rights will be observed in practice. Quite rightly, it establishes a link between civil liberties and access to the courts. If your rights and obligations—and thus the limits of your freedom—are at issue, you turn to the courts or are brought before them. Or if you think that your property rights are being undermined, your privacy invaded, that someone you have an agreement with is failing to abide by the terms, or if the authorities have deprived you of your liberty. In all such cases and in many others where a right is being infringed, you can apply to the courts. Some infringements are of course permissible. It may be necessary to search someone's home as part of a criminal investigation. A person with mental health problems may need to be committed to an institution in his or her own interests. But in these cases the executive—in criminal cases the prosecution service and the police—has to obtain permission from the courts.

In civil cases too, where the issue is often failure to abide by agreements, the possibility of recourse to the courts is crucial to the functioning of society. Otherwise the law of the jungle prevails. After all, if you have to give way to a stronger opponent and cannot appeal to a court, the result is that the most powerful and the most brazen will win, even if you, the weaker party, are convinced that you are right. That is the difference between being in the right and being proved right. Unfortunately, even if the court has made its ruling and decided you are in the right, you still have to wait for the other party to concede.

In Western democracies there is almost always an opportunity to bring a violation of the law, whatever its nature, before a court. Only in exceptional cases is this impossible. The option of appealing to an independent and impartial judge against the acts of the other branches

[2] Article 6, ECHR.
[3] Article 13, ECHR.

of government is a vital part of the rule of law. The courts have three essential functions.

1. Settling disputes and imposing penalties. The courts settle disputes on the basis of the law, decide whether a criminal offence has been committed and sentence convicted offenders, and impose sanctions or review sanctions imposed by administrative authorities. In coming to a decision, judges must disregard their own personal convictions and political preferences. People have to be able to rely on this.
2. Providing legal protection. In cases where the executive is involved, the courts review the lawfulness of the authorities' actions. This encourages government to abide by the law and offers legal protection to the individuals concerned. Providing legal protection also implies that, where necessary, the courts protect citizens from each other.
3. Judicial lawmaking. The courts interpret legislation. They contribute to lawmaking by explaining how the rules of law applicable to the cases before them should be understood.

Protecting human rights is the leitmotif running through these different functions. That is because in many countries human rights provisions in the Constitution have priority over other laws. In other countries, the Netherlands for example, the Constitution stipulates that the courts must always apply international provisions that have direct effect, such as the human rights provisions of the ECHR.

Nevertheless, for the courts to be able to carry out the three functions listed above, people have to be *able* to gain access to them. I shall return to the issue of access to the courts at the end of this chapter.

Just as important is the question of whether you *want* to bring a case before the courts. And you will not be inclined to do so if you suspect that the judges are not impartial, or if you think they will give the man who attacked your daughter or broke into your house a derisory sentence, or let him off altogether because of a procedural defect. Again, I shall come back to low sentences and procedural defects later on in this chapter. What I am concerned with here is that we must be able to trust our judges to apply the law correctly, otherwise the problem of people taking the law into their own hands arises.

The first precondition for trust in the judiciary is impartiality. Whether settling disputes between individuals or between individual citizens and government, judges must decide without bias. Their robes—worn in many countries by professional judges—symbolise their neutrality. And impartiality is so crucial to trust in the courts that the standard is extremely high: even the appearance of bias must be avoided. It must not be possible for either party to entertain a justified fear that the judge is prejudiced in favour of the other. See in this connection the section in Chapter 7 on recusal (challenge for bias).

The second precondition is independence. The executive must not exercise pressure on the judiciary. Judges must not have to fear for their position if they render judgments that are unwelcome to the government of the day. Which is why the prohibition on sacking judges is so essential. For the same reason I am absolutely opposed to the system in force in some states of the US, whereby judges are appointed for a limited period of time and then have to stand for re-election. Many chief justices of the state supreme courts I talked to at an international conference in Florence in December 2010 expressed the same view.

Independence from the executive is guaranteed by the way in which judges' legal status is regulated. Judges are in general appointed for life and can in the Netherlands only be dismissed by the Supreme Court on the application of the Procurator General (advisor to the Court). In the UK the possibility of dismissal also exists.

A concrete example of the independence of the judiciary in the Netherlands is the 2011 decision of the civil division of the Supreme Court in the Srebrenica case. The court ruled against the State. When I explained the ruling to an international audience consisting of members of the legal profession in Berlin, a Spanish attorney said: 'So you are really independent'. His admiration for something we Dutch take for granted is a vivid illustration of the fact that it is, after all, not so self-evident. In the history of the world we cannot point to many countries or to many periods in which there was a genuinely independent judiciary.

Although impartiality and independence are absolute preconditions for trust in a proper legal system, they sometimes mean that judges hand down rulings that are unwelcome to the general public. But judges must not be swayed by such considerations. Given the applicable law and given the particular circumstances, they will from time to time arrive at decisions which few will approve of. In such cases judges must remain steadfast and weather the storm until it dies down. In the grounds for the relevant decision they must demonstrate three things.

First, that they have identified the applicable law; second, that they have taken account of any margin for discretion; and third, that they have arrived at a just solution that takes account of all the circumstances of the case. This may sometimes be painful: rendering a tax measure null and void, or bringing a government plan to a halt, or acquitting a person many feel should have been convicted. In the words of French prosecutor Éric de Montgolfier, judges sometimes have the 'devoir de déplaire', the duty to displease.[4] The desire to please is the worst ailment a judge can suffer from.

Decisions that run counter to the sense of justice of a majority of the population can give rise to tension. And sometimes to a call to dismiss judges because their rulings are unwelcome. Such critics seem unaware of what would be lost if their call was heeded. As soon as a different majority wants something that would infringe *their* rights, they don't have a leg to stand on. A country where prevailing opinion is sufficient for rights to be trampled on is uncivilised.

And what about trial by jury? It has on occasion been suggested in the Netherlands, a country that has no jury system nor any lay element in its judiciary, that the introduction of trial by jury would increase people's trust in the legal system. The idea is that if people could see at first hand what happens in criminal proceedings and were able to make their own contribution to the process, their confidence in the system would increase.

Trial by jury exists in several Western democracies. It even existed in the Netherlands for a short period. A few months before Napoleon himself came to what was then the Kingdom of Holland in 1811, the country was incorporated into the French Empire and the French legal and administrative system was introduced. This meant that the Napoleonic Codes entered into force, including trial by jury in criminal proceedings. The jury had to decide whether a person was guilty on the basis of their *conviction intime* (inner conviction), rather than on the basis of statutory rules of evidence.[5]

In 1813, when the Netherlands was finally free of French rule, one of the first things to be abolished was trial by jury. It was never reinstated.

---

[4] Éric de Montgolfier, *Le devoir de déplaire*, Neuilly-sur-Seine, Éditions Michel Lafon, Paris 2006.

[5] See W H B Dreissen, *Bewijsmotivering in Strafzaken* (Evidence in Criminal Proceedings—in Dutch), The Hague, BJU, 2007, pp 11–12.

That is not to say that there has been no debate on the participation of laymen in legal proceedings. In 2006, Professor Theo de Roos was commissioned by the Minister of Justice, following questions in Parliament, to investigate whether such participation would increase the public's confidence in and understanding of the legal system.

Professor De Roos came to a number of interesting conclusions. First, he noted that countries are firmly attached to whatever system they have adopted, regardless of the degree or absence of lay participation. Second, there are advantages and disadvantages associated with each system. Better understanding by the public and greater democratic legitimacy are generally regarded as the most important advantages of lay participation. The disadvantages are that proceedings take longer and are more costly, while some believe that there are fewer quality safeguards.

He concluded that introducing lay participation was not the appropriate way to increase trust in the Dutch legal system. This is relatively strong in the Netherlands compared to other countries which do have some system of lay participation. De Roos therefore found there were no powerful arguments for its introduction in the Netherlands, while there was a strong argument against it: the costs that would be incurred. Radical and therefore expensive changes to criminal procedure would be required.[6]

If we look at the US, it would seem that trial by jury is so time-consuming that it has to be accompanied by a highly efficient 'grinder' that processes the bulk of criminal cases at high speed. In the US the vast majority of criminal cases are settled through plea bargaining, a system that comes in for a good deal of criticism. For example, because of the pressure exerted on defendants to confess and agree to a plea agreement, or the pressure on judges to settle a large number of cases and thus further restrict the already limited review they carry out of such agreements. For these reasons too, I believe the introduction of trial by jury would, generally speaking, undermine the quality of the rule of law in the Netherlands.

---

[6] Th A de Roos, *Is de invoering van lekenrechtspraak in de Nederlandse strafrechtspleging gewenst?* (Would it be desirable to introduce lay participation in Dutch criminal proceedings?—in Dutch), Tilburg University, 2006.

II. SETTLING DISPUTES AND IMPOSING PENALTIES

Traditionally, the judiciary comes into action in two situations. First, when individuals, institutions or companies are at odds with each other and fail to find a joint solution. The option they then have is to take their case to the courts. One of the parties to the conflict can do this against the will of the other, if necessary. This is the basis of the civil administration of justice: one of the parties applies to the civil courts, for example because the other party has failed to keep to the terms of a contract (to carry out proper renovations to a house, for instance) or has acted unlawfully in some other way (hit the other party with his car). According to article 17 of the Dutch Constitution, no one may be prevented from being heard by the courts against his will, a fundamental premise of the rule of law. Article 101 of the German Constitution states: 'No one may be removed from the jurisdiction of his lawful judge'. We have to be able to obtain redress from the courts. Of course, we can waive our right to do so or decide with the other party to resolve the matter in some other way, such as arbitration or mediation. But we are always free to apply to the courts. And they are obliged to decide one way or another. The courts cannot refuse to dispense justice. This can be concluded from article 6 of the ECHR, which states that courts must administer justice within a reasonable time. In the UK article 6, ECHR has internal effect, by virtue of the Human Rights Act 1998. In addition, in the Netherlands it can be concluded from the old General Legislative Provisions Act of 1829.

Disputes may also arise between an individual, institution or company on the one hand and government on the other. In the past, such disputes could be brought before the ordinary civil courts in the Netherlands. As of the beginning of the twentieth century, tax cases are heard by specialised tax divisions of the ordinary courts. Other administrative law cases are nowadays also heard at first instance by the district courts. On appeal they are heard by the Administrative Jurisdiction Division of the Council of State or by specialised appeal courts, like the appeal court for social security cases.

Another role played by the courts is to impose penalties or review penalties already imposed when someone has broken the law. In other words, this has nothing to do with settling disputes but with deciding on punishment. In the traditional criminal justice system, the public prosecutor lays the charges before the judge. Unlike in civil or administrative proceedings, this does not necessarily mean there is a conflict between the individual concerned and government. Defendants often confess to the crime with which they are charged. The court has to determine whether the charges are correct and if so, decide whether a penalty or what is known as a non-punitive measure—leaving aside the option of declaring the defendant guilty but waiving any sentence—is to be imposed. In such cases the judiciary acts as the 'strong arm' of government.

Nowadays, the imposition of penalties is gradually becoming the task of the executive as well. This includes the Public Prosecution Service. A considerable body of new legislation has empowered the executive to issue fines, for example. If an individual who has received such a fine does not respond, it becomes final and can be enforced. He or she can also take the matter to an administrative court, which will review whether the fine is lawful and appropriate. If a fine or an alternative sanction (community service, for instance, or a driving ban) imposed by the Public Prosecution Service is challenged, the case goes to the criminal courts, which play their traditional role. I will return to these developments and the questions they give rise to in Chapter 5.

III. ORGANISATION OF THE NATIONAL AND EUROPEAN COURTS

In many countries, the majority of cases are heard by what is called the court of first instance. If one of the parties disagrees with the ruling, they can apply to the court of appeal. And if they disagree with that ruling, they can often apply to the highest court in the land.

Alongside national jurisdictions we also have international courts. In Europe, two such courts play a substantial role in day-to-day legal practice at national level.

First, the Court of Justice of the European Union (CJEU—formerly known as the European Court of Justice), which sits in Luxembourg. Since the creation of the Common Market, the European Union and its predecessors have unleashed an avalanche of rules and regulations on its citizens, known under the collective title of the '*acquis commu- nautaire*'. The CJEU plays a major role in the interpretation of these rules. National courts in the EU can apply to the CJEU for a clear ruling on how to interpret EU law. If for example there is doubt about how a European provision on discrimination or on transport rules is to be understood, a national court faced with such an issue can submit what is known as a request for a preliminary ruling to the CJEU. The national court must take account of the CJEU's response when it decides on the matter. Lower courts have the option of submitting such a request where they need clarity, but the highest national courts, like the Supreme Court, are obliged to do so. The system ensures that European law is interpreted and applied in the same way throughout the EU. The CJEU may only concern itself with EU law, and therefore plays the leading role only in this circumscribed area.

Second, the European Court of Human Rights (ECtHR), located in Strasbourg. This court falls under the Council of Europe, a larger and much looser grouping of states including, for example, the Russian Federation, Moldova and Georgia, which operates alongside and sometimes overlapping the EU. The Council's most important document, binding on all its members, is the European Convention for the Protection of Human Rights and Fundamental Freedoms (ECHR). The ECtHR is the highest court overseeing compliance with the Convention and works in a very different way from the CJEU. Every individual in the Member States who believes that his or her human rights as laid down in the Convention have been violated can apply to the Court in Strasbourg, provided he or she has first exhausted all legal remedies available at national level and has found no redress. The Court may decide that this is indeed the case. Under article 41 of the Convention, the State concerned must then provide 'just satisfaction' to the injured party. In practice, if the Court decides there has been a violation of the Convention, this often means national courts have to make changes to their procedures, so that similar violations will not occur in the future. National courts must take heed of Court rulings: otherwise it will have constantly to rule on the same violations. And the system is not designed for that. It assumes that protection of the rights enshrined in the Convention is first and foremost the responsibility of the member states themselves. They have to put in place effective mechanisms to protect human rights and to offer redress if that protection fails in one way or another. Application to the Court in Strasbourg is meant to be a supplementary option; it only has to intervene if the national authorities have failed to fulfil their responsibilities.

In an ideal situation, all the Court would have to do is to lean back and note with some gratification that compliance with human rights is in order throughout the area under its jurisdiction. But that ideal will never be achieved. The legal and social reality in the Member States of the Council of Europe makes the individual legal protection offered by the Court indispensable.

In 1977 a commentator was able to say, without irony, that the Court 'had had a busy year because it had reached a decision in five cases'. At the time the Council had around 20 Member States. Since that year, the number of members and the Court's workload have increased dramatically. The Council now numbers 47 Member States, with a total population of around 820 million. All these states have recognised the right of individual petition to the Court. So an enforceable promise to respect their individual fundamental rights has been given to almost a billion people in an area stretching from Cyprus to the North Pole, and from Qaanaaq in north-western Greenland to Kamchatsky in the east of Russia. A glance at the overview of cases in the Court's annual report makes one thing very clear: serious violations of human rights still frequently occur in the countries of the Council of Europe and are insufficiently addressed by the national courts. Individual legal protection, as offered by the Court, is absolutely essential.

Partly because of this rapid expansion, the Court is struggling with an extremely heavy caseload. A former president of the Court, Sir Nicolas Bratza, describes the current burden of work as 'the inevitable consequence of the enlargement of the Council of Europe to include post-communist states as they embrace democracy'.[7]

The proper functioning of ECHR system is entirely dependent on the Member States' compliance with the Convention. If they fail to shoulder their responsibilities, or delay amendments to national legislation where ECtHR case law clearly indicates that this is necessary, the Court will be flooded with cases. At present, the Court needs all the support the member states can provide.

But then we may ask, does the Court take account of our views and opinions? I said earlier that the national courts must take heed of the Court's case law, but I would emphasise that 'take heed' does not mean 'follow slavishly'. Once the Court has rendered a leading judgment, each Member state has to decide whether and to what extent national

---

[7] See the speech given by President Bratza on 27 January 2012 at the opening of the ECtHR judicial year, published on the Court's website at www.echr.coe.int/Documents/Speech_20120127_Bratza_JY_ENG.pdf.

practice is in line with that judgment. Sometimes the national courts will have to adapt their case law in new cases dealing with the same matter (as happened as a result of the *Salduz v Turkey* case regarding access to a lawyer during police questioning). And sometimes the prosecuting authorities or the legislature will have to take swift action.

Loyalty to the Convention is not a unilateral issue. The Court pays considerable attention to the individual characteristics of the various Member States. They are not obliged to organise their legal systems in a uniform manner, as long as they provide a certain minimum level of human rights protection. The Court grants them a substantial 'margin of appreciation' (discretion), which is of crucial importance. If states get the impression that their room to manoeuvre at national level is being overly restricted, it can lead to vigorous protest. A prime example is the commotion in the UK over the cases involving prisoners' right to vote (in the UK they have no such right) and on the extradition of terrorist suspects to countries like Yemen (without assurances that they will receive a fair trial there). Or the case against Italy regarding crucifixes on the walls of classrooms in state schools. The ECtHR concluded in this case that it was not up to the Court to prohibit such symbols:

> The Court concludes in the present case that the decision whether crucifixes should be present in State-school classrooms is, in principle, a matter falling within the margin of appreciation of the respondent State. Moreover, the fact that there is no European consensus on the question of the presence of religious symbols in State schools speaks in favour of that approach.[8]

Aharon Barak, former president of the Israeli Supreme Court, once summarised the role of the judiciary as bridging 'the gap between law and life'. In other words, the courts have to weigh the interests involved in specific cases and arrive at a just solution. The rules of law should not stand in the way of this process, indeed they should facilitate it. What is regarded as reasonable and just differs from place to place and from time to time, and is shaped by national experience. As the French philosopher Blaise Pascal wrote: 'Vérité en deçà des Pyrénées, erreur au delà' ('There are truths on this side of the Pyrenees that are falsehoods on the other'). What others question, we find self-evident. In addition to this consideration, the answer to the question of what

---

[8] ECtHR, 18 March 2011, no. 30814/06 (*Lautsi v Italy*).

kind of approach is demanded by human rights practice in a particular country at a particular time can be very different according to the Member State concerned.

This is why in 1976 the ECtHR introduced the concept of the 'margin of appreciation' referred to above in connection with the case involving crucifixes in classrooms.[9] This concept concerns the margins within which national law can address compliance with the rights enshrined in the Convention. A good illustration is provided by the relatively recent (2010) case against Ireland involving the issue of abortion.[10]

In this case the Court explained its earlier case law on the issue of the margin of appreciation in the framework of article 8 of the Convention. Like other articles of the Convention, article 8 allows certain restrictions on the right it enshrines, namely the right to respect for private life, provided three conditions are met: the restrictions must be in accordance with the law, they must serve a legitimate aim referred to in the article and they must be necessary in a democratic society. The margin of appreciation concerns the room for assessment in answering that last question: is the restriction necessary in a democratic society?

The Court held that where a particularly important facet of an individual's existence or identity is at stake, the margin allowed to the state will normally be restricted. However, if there is no consensus within the Member States, either as to the relative importance of the interest at stake or as to the best means of protecting it, the margin will be wider. This is particularly the case where sensitive moral or ethical issues are involved. The Court noted that state authorities are, in principle, in a better position to give an opinion on the 'requirements of morals' in their country and what restrictions on rights under the Convention are necessary to meet them.

In this case the Court concluded that the Irish legislation on abortion was much more restrictive than that in other member states, but that Ireland had remained within the margin of appreciation.

---

[9] In the case ECtHR, 7 December 1976, no 5493/72 (*Handyside v UK*), para 48.
[10] ECtHR, 16 December 2010, no 25579/05 (*A, B and C v Ireland*).

IV. KEEPING THE DEBATE ON THE EUROPEAN COURT OF HUMAN RIGHTS TRANSPARENT

The issues discussed above sometimes become entangled in the current public debate. The case-load problem is seen, for example, as the fault of the Court itself. The argument is that it has adopted an overly broad interpretation of human rights and allows the Member States too narrow a margin of appreciation. What is more, it is argued that the Court should return to the intentions of the 'founding fathers' of the ECHR, along the lines of the doctrine of originalism (the view that the meaning of the US Constitution was fixed at the time of its enactment) in the US.

These are worrying developments. The willingness of Member State governments to resolve the case-load problem must never be dependent on a promise from the Court to interpret the Convention in a way acceptable to a particular government. If there is any area in which the saying 'he who pays the piper calls the tune' must not apply (either in theory or in practice), it is the administration of justice. In this context, Montesquieu's concept of the separation of powers is still absolutely up-to-date.

This kind of criticism also ignores the real reason for the workload: that too many human rights violations occur in the Member States. Added to which, the case law at issue is not clearly understood. In that case law the doctrine of the margin of appreciation is carefully explained and applied.[11] It often goes unrecognised that the Member States themselves have chosen to sign up to the various supplementary protocols and have explicitly confirmed that the Convention should be treated as a 'living instrument'.[12] As a result, the Court quite rightly regards it as its express obligation to interpret the Convention in light of present-day conditions.[13]

---

[11] See, eg, ECtHR, 6 October 2005 (Grand Chamber), no 74025/01 (*Hirst v UK*), and ECtHR, 16 December 2010, no 25579/05 (*A, B and C v Ireland*).

[12] On the occasion of the ratification of the EU Charter of Fundamental Rights of 7 December 2000, which has been legally binding since the Treaty of Lisbon entered into force in 2009.

[13] See as a random example, ECtHR, 7 January 2010, no 25965/04 (*Rantsev v Cyprus and Russia*).

Obviously, opinions on specific judgments vary and it is of course a good thing if every argument can be raised and discussed, as underlined by the dissenting opinions of ECtHR judges. But I believe that easy, generalising one-liners appealing to Eurosceptics that claim that the Court is assuming too much power and permits itself a scope for interpretation that the 'founding fathers' neither foresaw or intended have no real basis in what actually happens in the Court's practice. Nuances tend to be lost in the public and political debate. For example, the fact that the Court did not take the view that all British prisoners should be able to vote, only that a blanket, automatic loss of voting rights was incompatible with article 3 of Protocol 1. If you look at a cross-section of the case law in the Court's Annual Report, it is difficult to maintain that the Court is over-occupied with matters only distantly related to human rights.

We were aware that the great enlargement of the Council of Europe would present the Court with problems. But the task we are facing now is to tackle those problems together—practitioners, theorists and politicians. Even in economically difficult times, we should not be prepared to dilute the safeguards offered by the Convention. Shouldn't it be possible for the Court's work in guaranteeing human rights to cost a little more than the current €0.08 per head per year?[14]

V. ACCESS TO THE COURTS: FROM MAGNA CARTA TO APPLE V SAMSUNG

I referred earlier to article 17 of the Dutch Constitution and article 101 of the German Constitution, which state that no one may be prevented from being heard by the courts against his will, and article 6 of the European Convention on Human Rights which states that the courts must deliver a ruling within a reasonable time. 'Justice delayed is justice denied' is a legal maxim that dates at least from the time of Magna Carta.[15]

---

[14] The budget of almost €59 million referred to on pg 18 of the Court's 2011 Annual Report divided by the total population of the CoE Member States of around 819 million (pg. 155).

[15] Compelled by a group of rebel barons attempting to end his abuse of power, King John signed the charter at Runnymede on 15 June 1215. It guaranteed his vassals a number of rights.

Warren E. Burger, former Chief Justice of the US Supreme Court said in this context:

> A sense of confidence in the courts is essential to maintain the fabric of ordered liberty for a free people and three things could destroy that confidence and do incalculable damage to society:
>
> — that people come to believe that inefficiency and delay will drain even a just judgment of its value;
> — that people who have long been exploited in the smaller transactions of daily life come to believe that courts cannot vindicate their legal rights from fraud and over-reaching;
> — that people come to believe the law—in the larger sense—cannot fulfil its primary function to protect them and their families in their homes, at their work, and on the public streets.[16]

In 2014, we read in the media that HEMA, a Dutch department store chain, and wine-grower Ilja Gort resolved a dispute they had through amicable discussion. Gort took the view that a HEMA wine label bearing the image of a tulip was too similar to his labels. He complained to HEMA, which promised to change its labels. All's well that ends well. But in many cases things don't work out so swiftly and smoothly. Parties have completely opposing views, are not prepared—rightly or wrongly—to work towards a solution which involves compromise, and feel compelled to put their case before a court. In such cases it is extremely important that this option is open to them. Individuals and companies have to be able to call on an independent and impartial judiciary to settle their disputes with each other and with government, and to come to a well-considered decision based on expert knowledge.

Real access to the courts means that proceedings must not be too expensive, complicated or time-consuming. This is part of what philosophers call the 'social contract'. Citizens do not take the law into their own hands and they can be expected to abide by the rules laid down by government. In return, they must be able to apply to the courts if they believe they have suffered an injustice. Access to justice helps prevent vigilantism and adds to the legitimacy of government power.

Though not everyday routine, court rulings should be the most normal thing in the world. The principle of legal protection provided by an

---

[16] This quotation comes from a speech Burger gave to the American Bar Association on 10 August 1970, see Wikipedia under the reference 'Justice delayed is justice denied'.

independent and impartial judiciary is one of the fundamental premises of the rule of law. Most European politicians subscribe to this doctrine. In 2012, the Dutch Senate voted unanimously for a motion asking the government to introduce a new article in the Constitution establishing a general right to a fair trial before an independent and impartial judiciary. Many countries already have such a provision, constituting clear confirmation of the importance of access to the courts. Article 103 of the German Constitution states: 'In the courts every person shall be entitled to a hearing in accordance with law'.

In essence, access to the courts means that issues that seriously affect someone's legal position can be put before an independent judge. The matters involved are wide-ranging. Disputes between individuals or companies: from squabbles between neighbours to *Apple v Samsung*.[17] Or conflict with government not only when it imposes penalties, administrative or criminal: from a refusal to grant a residence permit to criminal proceedings involving death or manslaughter. And this access in cases involving the most minor to the most serious issues is not just fairly important, it is crucial. It is a fundamental aspect of the rule of law. Imagine the alternative: the garage that sold you a car two weeks ago denies that the crankshaft was rusted through and you have no legal remedy. Or the prosecutor says you are guilty of tax fraud and the fine imposed is a final decision.

But not every penalty has to be imposed by a court or is automatically reviewed by a court. Just think of the 10 million or so traffic fines imposed every year in the Netherlands. And in the field of civil law, the various alternatives to court proceedings are a good thing, and sometimes even more effective. Such alternatives must continue to be available, but should not be imposed on people. So it is acceptable for traffic fines to be largely automated, but there must always be a proper option to challenge them. The courts must not become a mirage we can see but never approach. A responsible system of access to the courts, in line with the principles of the rule of law, means that the greater the impact on a person's legal position, the fewer obstacles there must be to obtaining a judge's view on the matter and the more safeguards there must be to protect that process.

We thus have to remain alert to any restrictions on access to the courts. And these can take many forms. In boxer Mike Tyson's

---

[17] Case heard by The Hague District Court on 16 January 2013.

biography, for example, I read of a fairly unorthodox way to keep a case out of the criminal courts: by hiring the services of a 'hoodoo woman'. She told him to put $500 in a jar, to urinate in it and keep it under his bed for three days.[18] As the Roman Emperor Vespasian is claimed to have said, 'Pecunia non olet' (money doesn't stink).

It goes without saying that the legislature does not resort to such methods—which in Tyson's case, appear to have been ineffective. In the Western world, access to the courts is not, in practice, a question of all or nothing, rather of more or less. Which makes it liable to fluctuate. The degree to which it is available is directly connected with the degree to which the judiciary can perform the three functions I referred to earlier in this chapter: settling disputes and imposing penalties, while offering legal protection and contributing to the development of the law. The degree to which recourse to the courts for citizens and companies is a practical possibility is not only important as a remedy after the fact. It also throws a forward shadow, influencing the willingness of individuals, companies and institutions to abide by the law. Anyone who knows his opponent cannot just get his own way will tailor his conduct accordingly. The proper organisation of access to the courts is a guarantee of a decent society in which government—vis-à-vis citizens— and citizens—vis-à-vis each other—take account of the position and legitimate interests of others.

Amendments to legislation—leading for instance to a rapid rise in administrative fines—can affect the degree of access people have to the courts. But it is affected by other factors too. These are unrelated to the legislature and include quality considerations, costs, and the speed and complexity of court procedures. If proceedings are swift and not too expensive, applying to a court becomes more attractive and the courts become more accessible. In addition, people need to know that they will receive an expert opinion after a relatively straightforward procedure. The reverse is also true. The more costly, complex and time-consuming proceedings are, the less access is available. A complicating factor is that building in more safeguards to guarantee a good result virtually always increases costs, duration and complexity and places even higher demands on the judiciary. In organising access to the courts,

---

[18] Mike Tyson and Larry Sloman, *Undisputed Truth: My Autobiography*, Blue Rider Press, 2013.

the legislature also has to bear in mind that too high a threshold can prevent judges from properly performing their judicial tasks, while too low a threshold can open the gates to a flood of cases.

The effective organisation of access is therefore a complex and dynamic process. So many different influences are exerted by the various actors in this field: lawyers decide their fees and how they provide services, judges shape procedures and can make them more or less complicated, but it is the legislator who has the greatest impact. In the past few years, a huge variety of issues have occupied legal systems in the western world: court fees, the funding of legal aid, plans to introduced more digitalisation and specialisation in the administration of justice and efforts to achieve speedy disposal of cases. All of these have an influence on the degree of access people have to the courts.

To sum up, access to the courts costs time and money. And that is why its practical organisation rapidly becomes a contested issue, especially in times of austerity.

3

The Relationship between the Judiciary and the Legislature

... that in the night from 4 to 5 January 1909, the appellant, having been telephoned by Nijhof, did open a window in her house, yet when he informed her that the pipe had burst and asked her to turn the water off at the mains or to let him in so that he could do it, she firmly refused to comply with his request on the grounds that it was all nonsense intended to disturb her sleep and that they could come back the next day, in which refusal she persisted even when Nijhof said 'Think carefully about what you're doing, Miss, because this will lead to enormous damage'.[1]

THE ABOVE IS taken from a Dutch case which led to what is known as the Zutphen water mains judgment. A water pipe had burst in a storage unit for leather clothing. Because the occupant of the flat above refused to turn the water off at the mains, located in her home, the clothing was badly damaged. The question was where liability lay. In 1909, there was no statutory obligation for the occupant to take action to remedy the situation. The Supreme Court therefore decided her conduct was not unlawful. The ruling ran counter to many people's sense of justice and attracted considerable criticism.

I. NOT JUST THERE TO APPLY THE LAW

At the beginning of the twentieth century, courts in the Netherlands were chiefly concerned with applying the law. If this sometimes led to an unreasonable outcome, there was little the judiciary could do about it. The 1910 Zutphen water mains ruling is a prominent example. But from the early twentieth century onwards, the Dutch Supreme Court gradually began to change its approach, influenced by public criticism

---

[1] Dutch Supreme Court, 10 June 1910, W9038.

and the younger judges joining its ranks. The assessment of whether there had been a 'violation of the law' began to evolve, as illustrated by the 1919 Lindenbaum-Cohen ruling.[2] Cohen was a printer in Amsterdam who bribed a man working for his competitor, Lindenbaum, to pass on information about Lindenbaum's quotations for work (what we nowadays call industrial espionage). But at the time it was not defined as an offence in the law. The Supreme Court ruled that what Cohen had done was nevertheless unlawful, on the grounds that it was incompatible with 'the due care that should be exercised with regard to another's person or property'. This was an important step, in line with public opinion, that reduced the gap between the law and justice.

The interaction between public opinion and the justice system became more direct. Different ways of making the administration of justice take account of developments in society were created. The legislature came to see this as desirable, and followed the judiciary. What might be called 'open norms' were built into legislation, general standards that have to be fleshed out in practice. Just think of concepts like 'urgent necessity' or 'reasonable time'. What these mean is for the courts to decide. Consequently, justice is embodied not only in laws that are applied by the courts, but also in interpretation of those laws or of treaties by the courts. This is known as judicial lawmaking and is the subject of this chapter. How far can the courts go in this process? They are obliged to reach balanced solutions within the framework of the law in the cases brought before them, but they must not step into the shoes of the legislature.

II. THE DEMOCRACY PRINCIPLE AND JUDGES' PERSONAL OPINIONS

And judicial use of the 'will of the reasonable legislator'—even if at times it is a fiction—helps statutes match their means to their overall public policy objectives, a match that helps translate the popular will into sound policy. An overly literal reading of a text can too often stand in the way.[3]

---

[2] Dutch Supreme Court, 31 January 1919.
[3] S Breyer, *Active Liberty: Interpreting Our Democratic Constitution*, New York, Alfred A. Knopf, 2006, p 101.

The courts function within a democracy. This means that the legislature determines the broad organisation of the state and society. That was always my guiding principle as President of the Dutch Supreme Court. You could call it the 'democracy principle'. It implies that the courts must exercise restraint when presented with matters involving the organisation of the state. They must always come to a decision, but sometimes a cautious one. The doctrines of 'judicial restraint' and 'political question' point in the same direction: the courts must not overplay their hand and must refrain, except where it is impossible, from interfering in choices that should be made by government and legislature. For example, it would be inappropriate for the courts to give their own view on what the maximum personal excess should amount to in healthcare insurance: this is a matter for the legislature.

What also follows from the democracy principle is that in interpreting the law, the courts first examine the original vision of the legislators. That is why the Dutch Supreme Court (like other courts with a major lawmaking role) relies heavily on the explanatory memorandum accompanying a piece of legislation and the debate in parliament during its passage. The more recent the legislation in question, the heavier that reliance. An historical interpretation of law—focusing on what the maker of that law intended—is thus important.

If a court has to interpret a law and does not find in the accompanying documents any evidence of what the legislator would have wanted to see in a case such as that now before it, the sensible course is for the court to ask itself what a reasonable legislator would decide. It tries to put itself in the position of the legislature in relation to the public policy objective it was attempting to achieve (known as teleological interpretation). But the democracy principle goes further. Even if the text of the law seems clear, the court still has to ask itself what the lawmakers intended. The quotation above comes from a book by associate justice of the US Supreme Court, Stephen Breyer and it favours the interpretation method based on an imaginary legislator and his objectives over literal interpretation.

To illustrate, the following is a case in which the Dutch Supreme Court was confronted with an illegal intercountry adoption. The defendant was accused of transporting a child aged around one from Brazil to the Netherlands with the intention of placing it with a Dutch couple outside of the official adoption procedure. The offence in question is defined in article 278 of the Dutch Criminal Code, which reads:

> Anyone who transports someone across the frontier of the Netherlands in Europe, with the aim of unlawfully placing him under the control of another person or of transporting him in a state of helplessness, is guilty of kidnapping and as such liable to a term of imprisonment not exceeding twelve years or a fifth-category fine.

The history of this article's passage through parliament in the 1880s indicated that the intention was to provide protection against the white female slave trade. The trade brought about long-term deprivation of women's liberty through transportation to a foreign country whose language they did not speak, and put them beyond the reach of the Dutch authorities. This was not the case in the proceedings in question. There was no question of transporting a person *out of* the country but rather *into* the Netherlands. Nevertheless, the Supreme Court applied the article to the illegal adoption, even though at the time the article was enacted, the legislator had been concerned with transportation out of the country. The Court took the view that, taken as a whole, applying the article to transportation into the country did not run counter to the text of the law. It stated:

> The changes in circumstances and generally accepted opinion that have taken place since this criminal provision entered into force mean that there is now no reasonable ground in applying the article for drawing a distinction, counter to its formulation, between the kinds of protection provided in the two cases the Court has just referred to.[4]

The highest court in the Netherlands thus implicitly attempted to determine what the reasonable legislator in 2001 would think of the criminalisation of irregular intercountry adoption. It added new content to the text of the law, at least in comparison to the explanation given by the legislature in the 1880s.

One result of observing the democracy principle is that the Dutch Supreme Court regularly establishes that a particular matter falls outside the courts' lawmaking powers. In other words, the choices to be made demand direct democratic legitimation by the legislature. There is widespread support for this approach, whereby the Supreme Court

---

[4] Dutch Supreme Court, 20 November 2001.

provides solutions where it can, at the same time demonstrating its awareness that the broad organisation of the state and society, as well as major questions in this respect, do not fall within its competence.

A recent example of this is the question of the right to legal assistance during police questioning. The argument was that there should be a general right to have a lawyer present at this stage. The Dutch Supreme Court reasoned as follows.

> In view of the policy, organisational and financial aspects involved, drafting such a general regulation of legal assistance when a suspect is being questioned by police goes beyond the lawmaking task of the Supreme Court. [...]. It is therefore the responsibility of the legislator to introduce a statutory provision regulating such assistance as soon as possible. The possibility cannot be excluded that the continued absence of such a provision will at some point lead to a different assessment of future cases in which questions regarding the content and scope of the right to legal assistance during police questioning are brought before the Supreme Court.[5]

Judges must not translate their personal preferences into legal opinions. That was the charge levelled at the US Supreme Court by Billings Learned Hand when from 1914 onwards the Court became consistently hostile to President Theodore Roosevelt's legislation on social reform. As Gerald Gunther remarked, 'The Court had returned to its pattern of transforming personal biases into constitutional doctrine'.[6] The judiciary is not granted independence in order for it to propagate its personal opinions. Judges must try to factor developments and changes in society into their judgments. In the Netherlands this trend has been visible in the changes related to the concept of self-defence in criminal law. People now have more scope for defending themselves against someone acting unlawfully towards them than twenty years ago. The message now is that citizens don't have to stand by and accept everything.

Judicial independence is there to enable the courts to operate free of temporary political majorities or prevailing public opinion. Judges must even be able to disregard any powerful religious, political or other convictions they may have. That this is not pure theory is evidenced

---

[5] Dutch Supreme Court, 1 April 2014.

[6] G Gunther, *Learned Hand, the Man and the Judge*, Oxford University Press, 2010, p 211.

by the case law on euthanasia in the Netherlands. The possibility of terminating a person's life in certain circumstances without being prosecuted was created in 1984 by the Criminal Division of the Supreme Court, a majority of whose judges were Catholics and thus were going against the teachings of the Church.

III. INTERPRETING THE LAW? NAPOLEON'S DISTRESS

Montesquieu had a clear opinion on the courts' lawmaking task: it did not exist. For him, the judge was simply the mouthpiece of the legislator. *'Le juge est la bouche de la loi'* is possibly the most quoted sentence in the legal literature from then on.

> It is possible that the law, which is clear sighted in one sense, and blind in another, might, in some cases, be too severe. But as we have already observed, the national judges are no more than the mouth that pronounces the words of the law, mere passive beings, incapable of moderating either its force or rigor.[7]

Well over 250 years later, there is more to be said about judicial lawmaking than this. Look at the heated debates in the US on this subject, more precisely on the role of federal Supreme Court judges. Controversial decisions on issues such as abortion or same-sex marriage continue to arouse strong emotions. There are representatives of the different schools of thought in the Supreme Court: Justice Breyer and the late Justice Scalia, for example, are well-known for their opposing views on the role of the courts in interpreting the US Constitution. Breyer considers the Constitution to be a living instrument, a document whose wording may perhaps not be literally applied to situations and cases that its framers could not have foreseen over 200 years ago but which can be applied through interpretation by the courts. Scalia on the other hand saw himself as an 'originalist', someone who thinks the Constitution should be interpreted in accordance with the text and original meaning. New, unforeseen situations should, in his view, be decided on by a democratically elected body.

In practice however, these opposing views are not always so sharply delineated. Scalia once said that most originalists are 'faint-hearted' and

---

[7] Montesquieu, *The Spirit of Laws*. 1748. Translated by Thomas Nugent, 1750.

most non-originalists 'moderate'.[8] This may explain why at the public hearing of the US Senate Judiciary Committee referred to in Chapter 1, Scalia and Breyer broadly agreed on the role of the Supreme Court. Scalia fully agreed with the observation of former associate justice Louis Brandeis that 'The most important thing that we do is doing nothing', though Breyer questioned whether it was the *most* important.

That would have been music to Napoleon's ears. According to tradition, when confronted with commentaries on his civil code he exclaimed 'Mon code est perdu' (My code is lost). He took the view that the courts had manipulated his legislation, undermining equality before the law, legal uniformity, and—possibly the most worrying aspect for Napoleon—the power of the legislature.

In practice, this may be unavoidable for courts aiming to arrive at reasonable solutions in concrete cases. For example, an agreement may stipulate that a contractor will install a fireplace with an opening based on the client's preferred dimensions. It then transpires that the chimney is too narrow to create a sufficient draught with an opening of that size. First the court has to establish what exactly the parties agreed. It must then assess the contractor's defence that the client insisted on that size of opening. The client may respond that as the technical expert, the contractor should have warned him that the chimney might not draw well given the discrepancy between the narrow flue and the large opening. This amounts to more than just applying a legal provision which says that agreements must be complied with.

Let's take another example, this time from the criminal law. As we know, theft is a criminal offence. But what about someone who observes another person withdrawing money from a cash machine and manages to see her PIN code. He then steals the cash and the debit card, and then withdraws money from the person's bank account. What offence has been committed here? The Dutch Criminal Code says: 'Anyone who removes any good belonging wholly or partially to any other person with the intention of unlawfully appropriating it is guilty of theft'. And this offence is aggravated if 'false keys' are used to commit it. The article is based on the idea of one person physically taking something from another, and the term 'false keys' was introduced long

---

[8]   A. Scalia, 'Originalism, The Lesser Evil', 1988, in D. M. O'Brien (ed.), *Judges on Judging, Views from the Bench*, Washington, CQ Press, 2008, p 198–206.

before debit cards with PIN codes were invented. This example also gives rise to the question of who has been robbed? The bank or the account holder? And has the money in the account been stolen, or just the debit card? Is a debit card in the hands of a thief a 'false key'? Here too, the court cannot simply apply the legal provision to the case at hand. In the law of England and Northern Ireland theft is defined as 'the dishonest appropriation of property belonging to another with the intention of permanently depriving the other of it.' On the facts given above, the taker would have committed (i) theft of the bank card (unless, as is unlikely, he meant to give it back), (ii) theft of the notes, belonging to the bank, that he withdrew from the ATM machine and (iii) theft of the victim's bank account.

The ideal of courts applying the law, word for word, to the facts in question—if it ever existed in reality—has vanished. But this was inevitable. The legislator is simply unable to foresee everything and regulate every possible situation in advance. To an increasing extent, loopholes in the law have to be repaired and the courts are being asked to adjudicate on a growing number of politically charged issues.[9] Through the use of open norms, as outlined earlier, and interpretation methods other than the purely literal, the legislative remit of the courts has expanded.[10] It can encompass both minor points as well as major issues, such as the decision as to whether a certain kind of behaviour is unlawful, as in the Lindenbaum-Cohen case outlined above.

Quite apart from the need for restraint vis-à-vis the legislature, the question of lawmaking by the courts has other inherent complications. Legal certainty demands that the rules of law be clear and precise, so those to whom they apply know what can be expected of them. However, the exact significance of many rules of law only becomes clear in case law. When these rules are applied in specific cases, the exact content of the law becomes known to all. This is not ideal from

[9] S K Martens, 'De Grenzen van de rechtsvormende taak van de rechter' (The limits of judicial lawmaking—in Dutch), in *Trema*, 2000, no 5, p 174, ascribing this development to 'political powerlessness'. The trend is perceptible in many other democratic states governed by the rule of law. See, eg, Ran Hirschi, *Towards Juristocracy. The Origins and Consequences of the New Constitutionalism*, Cambridge Massachusetts and London, Harvard University Press, 2004, p 15.

[10] G J Wiarda, *Drie typen van rechtsvinding* (Three types of judicial lawmaking—in Dutch), W E J Tjeenk Willink, fourth impression, 1999, pp 36–40.

the perspective of the foreseeability of the law, but there is little that can be done about it. The European Court of Human Rights ruled some time ago that the requirement of foreseeability does not stand in the way of the development of the law through judicial interpretation.[11]

The administration of justice must serve the interests of society. Any Supreme Court judge who systematically ignored technological progress and ruled, for instance, just simply that stealing electricity or virtual objects was not foreseen by the legislator and therefore falls outside the scope of the criminal law, has misunderstood his task. He might indeed even be acting contrary to the spirit of article 17 of the Dutch Constitution and Article 101 of the German Constitution (as discussed in Chapter 2).

From time to time the courts have to make law in very sensitive matters. And sometimes the legislature takes the court's solution and incorporates it in a new law. This is known as codification of case law. An example is the wording of the Lindenbaum-Cohen judgment, incorporated in the definition of an unlawful act in article 162 of Book 6 of the Dutch Civil Code. Another is the Dutch legislation on euthanasia, which is in fact based on a series of Supreme Court judgments. These are two fine examples of 'Montesquieu in reverse': the legislator takes the words of the judiciary and makes them its own.[12]

The old view of the position and role of the judge, as expressed by Montesquieu in the passage cited earlier, is no longer in line with current insights and court practice. The judiciary has gradually acquired a greater remit than that allowed it by the French political philosopher.

IV. NO REFUSAL TO ADJUDICATE: EUTHANASIA
AND LEGISLATORS WHO DRAG THEIR FEET

'The judge who refuses to give judgment, claiming that the law is silent, opaque or insufficient, may be prosecuted for refusal to adjudicate.' This comes from section 13 of the Dutch General Legal Provisions

---

[11] See ECtHR, *C.R. v the United Kingdom*, 22 November 1995, no. 20190/92.

[12] G J M Corstens, *Prudence et audace* (Caution and daring—in Dutch), address on my inauguration as President of the Dutch Supreme Court, *Nederlands Juristenblad* 2013, p 1098.

Act of 1829, which despite its age, is still on the statute books and embodies an important principle. Judges must give judgment. If two parties cannot resolve a dispute themselves, they can apply to the court, which cannot refuse to hear the case. In the UK there is no such legal provision. But a judge in the lower courts who refused to give judgment would probably be dismissed for misconduct; and in the case of a High Court Judge, such conduct might, in theory, lead to Parliament's requesting the Queen to dismiss him or her. The legislature can postpone decision-making, the judiciary cannot. Section 13 is thus a fixed standard, consolidated by the requirement contained in article 6 of the European Convention on Human Rights that in civil and criminal cases the courts must decide within a reasonable time. Article 6 does not mention administrative cases, but in the Netherlands the Supreme Court (in tax cases) and the Administrative Jurisdiction Division of the Council of State (administrative law cases) have now attached sanctions to failure to observe this limit in administrative proceedings.

The world of politics sometimes fails to find solutions to difficult problems, or fails to find them fast enough. If the courts are then confronted with a case involving such a problem, they have to give an answer. This is what happened in the Netherlands in connection with termination of life on request and assisted suicide (grouped here together under the term euthanasia). Article 293 of the Dutch Criminal Code makes the first a criminal offence, article 294 the second. The last three decades of the twentieth century witnessed a fierce debate on whether such acts should be punished. While the debate was going on, case law was established that allowed a certain amount of scope for euthanasia. The Supreme Court turned to the old concept of necessity to establish that a doctor's criminal liability for such acts might under certain circumstances be waived if he acted from necessity. In a series of judgments, the Court developed criteria to assess if such a situation was at issue.[13] In cases of euthanasia, the court must investigate whether the doctor made a sound choice between conflicting obligations—the duty to keep the patient alive and the duty to relieve his or her suffering.

Ultimately, the Supreme Court decided that intolerable suffering without prospect of improvement that had a physical cause could justify

---

[13]   Dutch Supreme Court 27 November 1984, 21 October 1986 and 21 June 1994.

euthanasia. Later, in 1994, the Supreme Court stated that suffering caused by a recognised mental illness or disorder might also justify terminating a patient's life. But it established a limit: in a following case involving not a recognised mental or physical disorder but a patient who was 'finished with life', the Court said euthanasia was not justified.

Judicial lawmaking is not just a consequence of the ban on refusing to adjudicate. What is known as the 'juridification of society' has also contributed to its growth. Laws and treaties have to be interpreted and the significance of European case law for each Member State's legal order has to be explained. The highest courts play a key role in this process, since the lower courts apply to them for interpretation. Efficiency considerations too mean the lower courts have a greater need for Supreme Court case law they can follow.

The Dutch Supreme Court has adopted a method to provide clarity to lower courts: it publishes overviews of judgments on a specific theme.[14] Another method is to hand down speedy rulings on new legislation that plays a role in a large number of cases[15] or in other cases that require a swift response.[16] Think for example of the ABN-AMRO case (concerning a large bank), where the key issue was the powers of a company's board of directors versus those of the general meeting of shareholders. The Advocate-General (advisor to the Supreme Court) produced an advisory opinion and the Court handed down its ruling in a short space of time.[17] The tax sector provides another illustration: a case on the fees to be paid for an identity card.[18] The Supreme Court ruled that there was no sufficient statutory basis for such fees, a loophole which the legislator rapidly repaired.

---

[14] For eg, on the reasonable time requirement in tax cases (Supreme Court 22 April 2005) and in criminal proceedings (17 June 2008); on art 359a (breach of procedural rules) of the Code of Criminal Procedure (30 March 2004) and on measures of constraint under the law of criminal procedure (28 September 2010).

[15] For eg, on art 359, para 2 (grounds for judgment) of the Code of Criminal Procedure (Dutch Supreme Court 11 April 2006), or on s 80a (cassation) of the Judiciary (Organisation) Act (11 September 2012).

[16] For eg, the ABN-AMRO case referred to below, or the Lehman Brothers case (Dutch Supreme Court, 1 March 2013).

[17] Dutch Supreme Court, 13 July 2007.

[18] Dutch Supreme Court, 9 September 2011.

Below I shall discuss a number of cases in which the courts played a lawmaking role.

'Teen steals virtual items, gets real punishment' was how CBS News summarised a 2012 Dutch Supreme Court judgment on the question of whether stealing a virtual mask and amulet in Runescape, an online game, could be considered as theft of goods within the meaning of article 310 of the Criminal Code, which came into force in 1886.

V. TECHNOLOGICAL ADVANCES, VIRTUAL THEFT AND FLOCK FIBRES

Though the point of law involved in the Runescape case was an interesting one, the facts were disturbing. Together with another boy, the defendant had beaten a thirteen-year-old boy and threatened him with a knife in order to compel him to 'drop' the two virtual objects in the game. The other thief could then pick up the items, making them his virtual property.

The grounds given by the Supreme Court for its judgment were considerably longer than CBS's summary:

3.3.1.   The grounds for appeal pose the question of whether virtual objects such as this can be regarded as 'goods' within the meaning of article 310 of the Criminal Code. When article 310 was introduced in 1886, the legislature could not, obviously, take account of this question. Nor has it ever arisen in the case law of the Supreme Court. Nevertheless, both the law and earlier case law provide a basis for answering the question now before the Court.

3.3.2.   Through a variety of criminal provisions, the legislature has aimed to protect the rightful owner's right to dispose of his goods. Article 310 of the Criminal Code makes it an offence to remove any good belonging to another person from his effective control with the intention of unlawfully appropriating it. The concept of a 'good' has an independent significance under the criminal law. It can embrace non-material objects as well, provided that the object, by its nature, can be removed from the effective control of another person.

3.3.3.   Over the years, the Supreme Court has answered several questions regarding the interpretation of the term 'good', including with regard to other provisions containing this concept. Its ruling of 23 May 1921, p. 564 concerned the question of whether electricity could be regarded as a 'good' within the meaning of article 310. That question was answered in the affirmative. The Court held that it could not be denied that electrical energy possessed 'a certain independent existence'. Other considerations were that electricity could be generated and controlled by human beings, and 'represented a certain value, on the one hand because of the cost and effort associated with its acquisition, on the other because human beings are able to use it either for their own benefit or to supply it to others for remuneration'. These considerations led to the conclusion that 'since article 310 aims to protect the property of another, and in pursuance of that aim defines as a criminal offence the removal of any good under the circumstances listed in the article without in any way defining what should be included under the heading 'any good', the article applies to electricity on the basis of the characteristics listed above'.

In a Supreme Court judgment of 11 May 1982 concerning article 321 of the Criminal Code, which makes embezzlement a criminal offence, the question arose of whether funds being transferred electronically could be regarded as a good belonging to another person, and therefore susceptible of being misappropriated. The Supreme Court concluded that a reasonable interpretation of article 321 led to an affirmative answer, 'in view of the function of electronic funds transfers in society'.

Further, the Court has ruled that the retention in a person's memory of the digits making up his or her PIN code cannot be regarded as a 'good' within the meaning of article 317 of the Criminal Code and informing another person (voluntarily or involuntarily) about a PIN code cannot be considered as 'surrender' within the meaning of the article; 'surrender' only takes place if the person surrendering the item in question thereby loses the item (cf. Supreme Court 13 June 1995).[19]

On the basis of these considerations, the Court came to the conclusion that an act of theft of this kind came within the scope of the relevant article of the Criminal Code.

If an act is not defined as an offence at the time that it is committed, the perpetrator cannot be prosecuted for it. This principle—known as the legality principle—is so important that the Dutch Criminal Code enshrines it in its very first article and the French Criminal

---

[19] Dutch Supreme Court, 31 January 2012.

Code devotes its second and third article to this rule. But the world is evolving at a furious pace and, as we saw earlier, the legislature cannot foresee everything. Given these facts, how can we prevent loopholes developing in legislation without making it so elastic that practically everything falls within its scope?

What we need are definitions that allow room for unforeseen cases to be included. The legislature must not try to define all possible concrete situations in advance but rather describe a type of behaviour that should be penalised. Subsequently, the courts decide in the cases brought before them whether the matter at hand falls within a particular definition of a crime. The Runescape case is a typical example. In the quotation above the Supreme Court referred to a renowned case dating from 1921, the 'electricity' case. At the time, the theft of electricity was new: the authors of the Criminal Code could not have envisaged it in 1886. The same thing happened at the end of the 1970s when the computer began its inexorable rise. Fairly quickly electronic funds transfers became possible, giving rise to the question of whether money transferred in this way could be misappropriated. Again, the answer was not in the legislation, and so the Supreme Court had to decide on the theft of virtual items.

In doing so, it was acting as a lawmaker, adapting the law to new technology without the intervention of the legislature. If it had not done so, it would have abandoned the public, in particular the victims of the manipulation of new technology, to their fate. Of course, the Court could have reasoned as follows: if we interpret the law according to the letter, we will compel the legislature to act swiftly. Classing the new situation under existing legislation solves the problem as far as the legislature is concerned, so it takes no action.

But the Supreme Court opted for a broad interpretation and as a result, virtual objects can be regarded as 'goods' within the meaning of the 1886 provisions on theft. Even though the nineteenth-century legislators had not foreseen this development, the Court's choice was not incompatible with the principle of legality—in the case of theft, what matters is the fact of stealing; what you steal is a secondary consideration.

This is but one example. The courts are constantly confronted with questions arising from the advance of technology. In the criminal law sphere, for instance, there is the question of whether breaches of individual rights through the use of new technology are permissible in investigating criminal offences. The methods involved range from observation using thermal imaging cameras (to detect cannabis factories) to the interception of various forms of communication (from telephone to WhatsApp).

In 2013 two cases involved the permissibility of what is called the 'flock-fibre method',[20] and of 'stealth text messages', sent to a mobile phone user to locate his whereabouts.[21] The flock-fibre method was used in a case where several persons were suspected of committing robberies. Because it was difficult to observe the persons in question using currently permissible methods, the interior of a car belonging to one of them was treated with a spray containing fibres. The aim was to be able to verify whether the driver and passengers had been at the scene of the crime by identifying the fibres they were shedding. The defendants' lawyers argued that the method infringed their clients' right to privacy under article 8 of the European Convention on Human Rights, since it makes it possible to trace a person's movements. If that is so, the court must decide whether such an invasion of privacy is justified on the grounds that it is in accordance with the law and necessary in a democratic society to serve the interests listed in article 8, paragraph 2 (which include the prevention of crime). This was the legal framework that had to be applied to the use of the flock-fibre method.

These questions are important from the perspective of the rule of law, since they impose limits on the use of criminal investigation techniques. In turn, this sets boundaries on the actions of the police and criminal justice authorities, in order to safeguard the freedom of each and every one of us. The investigation system is, after all, based on the idea that the criminal justice authorities may not do everything that either is or seems to be useful. To protect individual freedoms, the authorities too are subject to limits. Technology makes many things possible, but does not legitimise them all. Though in fact, the Supreme Court did decide the flock fibre method and stealth texting were permissible.

Another issue that new technology raises for the courts is the value of evidence acquired through the newest methods. The priority here

---

[20] Dutch Supreme Court, 3 May 2013.
[21] Dutch Supreme Court, 1 July 2013.

is establishing the truth, but a dilemma presents itself. On the one hand, new methods that produce reliable evidence cannot of course be ignored. On the other, the risk that someone is convicted on the basis of unreliable evidence must always be avoided.

In the recent past, we have seen a number of success stories in this respect: advances in DNA techniques have made it possible to identify and bring to trial people suspected of 'cold' crimes years later. Paternity and other family relationships are easier to establish. But we have also had to learn some hard lessons. For instance, the errors made by a Dutch police team in carrying out scent-identification tests with detector dogs. When it emerged that the protocol governing such tests had been regularly breached, it discredited the reliability of hundreds of these tests. The prosecuting authorities notified all defendants in whose cases scent identification might have played a role and informed them that they could apply to the Supreme Court for a retrial if their sentence had become final and unappealable. Or take the case of the nurse, Lucia de Berk, who was initially sentenced to life imprisonment for murdering patients. It later emerged that her conviction was not supported by the evidence, which was largely based on medical and statistical findings. After the Supreme Court had reviewed her case, she was ultimately acquitted. The case gave rise to a debate on the question of whether legal professionals (attorneys, prosecutors and judges) understand expert witnesses and their testimony sufficiently well. After a successful experiment in which forensic experts were seconded to three district courts, the possibility of appointing such an expert at each district court is under consideration.[22]

VI. SOCIAL DEVELOPMENTS: FRENCH KISSING, REPUDIATION AND WRONGFUL LIFE

The Dutch Supreme Court knows everything, officially speaking, about French kissing. In the first 'French kiss judgment', handed down in 1998, the Court determined that French kissing an unwilling person

---

[22] 'Forensische ondersteuning helpt strafrechters' (Forensic support helps criminal judges—in Dutch), *Nederlands Juristenblad* 2013, p 1098.

amounted to rape.[23] Article 242 of the Dutch Criminal Code defines rape as follows: 'by means of violence or other means or threat of violence or other means, compelling another person to submit to an act which includes or constitutes physical penetration'. In the second 'French kiss judgment', the Court came to a different conclusion.[24] It gave a number of grounds for this change of course. It pointed out that the first judgment had from the start encountered criticism in the professional literature and was not always followed by the lower courts. The critics stated that defining a French kiss as rape was not in line with normal use of language and went beyond the boundaries of the concept of rape, while article 246 of the Criminal Code, which makes it an offence to compel another person to commit or submit to an indecent act, could equally and more appropriately have been applied. A conviction for rape in these circumstances would be perceived as wrong and unjust, because a French kiss cannot, in all reasonableness, be equated with sexual intercourse or an equivalent act. Furthermore, the maximum sentence for rape (12 years' imprisonment) is considerably higher than that carried by an offence under article 246 (8 years' imprisonment). Finally, the Supreme Court noted that having the word 'rape' on a person's criminal record would have much more serious social repercussions than a less loaded term.

And so, through case law, social as well as technological developments have their effect on the law. The French kiss rulings are a prime example. The social climate in which the first judgment was handed down was very different from that in 2013. Heated debate on rape and the position of women played a much greater role in 1998 and new legislation on sexual offences had been introduced only seven years before, without 'French kissing' having been explicitly mentioned in the notes explaining the text.

Family law is another branch where social developments give rise to questions of law. For example, a man with dual Moroccan/Dutch nationality who had been living in the Netherlands for many years married a Moroccan woman in that country. They lived together for a while in the Netherlands, then she returned to Morocco, where she was repudiated, at her own request, by her husband. This form of dissolution

[23] Dutch Supreme Court, 24 April 1998.
[24] Dutch Supreme Court, 12 March 2013.

of a marriage under Moroccan law (known as *khoel*) takes place in the presence of two public officials designated as witnesses (*adoul*) by the authorities. A certificate known as the *acte de répudiation compensatoire* is drawn up, signed by the witnesses and then confirmed by a magistrate hearing notarial cases (notary *Qadi*) of this kind. The registrar of births, deaths and marriages in the Netherlands refused to enter the certificate as proof of dissolution in the municipal personal records database. The man asked the district court to order the official to register the certificate, and the court complied with his request.

When the case went to the Supreme Court, it established that both husband and wife had Moroccan nationality and the dissolution of the marriage was valid under Moroccan law. What is more, the wife had consented to the dissolution. It was also in her interests for the dissolution to be recognised in the Netherlands as well as in Morocco. For that reason, the Court concluded that the dissolution, even though it was based on repudiation, should be recognised.[25]

A difficult moral and social dilemma was presented by the case of baby Kelly.[26] She was born severely disabled as a result of chromosomal defects. Prenatal testing would have revealed the defects, but the midwife failed to carry out such tests, even though the mother wanted them. This was incompatible with the midwife's duty of care and consequently unlawful. On these grounds, Kelly and her parents sued the hospital where she was born and the midwife for damages. The Supreme Court had decided in an earlier case that parents whose child had been born as the result of a mistake made by a doctor in treatment to prevent another pregnancy were entitled to compensation to cover the costs of caring for and raising the child in question.[27] The Court extended this line of reasoning in the case of baby Kelly. What was new about the ruling was that it decided that the parents could also apply for damages for pain and suffering. In the Dutch legal system, a mother's right to terminate a pregnancy is recognised, within certain limits, and in the baby Kelly case these limits had not been exceeded. This is based on a woman's fundamental right of self-determination, to decide what happens with her own body. If an error made by a midwife means

---

[25] Dutch Supreme Court, 13 July 2001.
[26] Dutch Supreme Court, 18 March 2005.
[27] Dutch Supreme Court, 21 February 1997.

that a woman was unable to choose to prevent the birth of a severely disabled child, there has been a serious breach of that right.

VII. INTERPRETING NEW LEGISLATION: STALKING AND PEEPSHOWS

With respect to the defendant it is found proven that:

> in the period from 1 October 2000 to 12 July 2001 he unlawfully, systematically and intentionally invaded the privacy of X (the victim), with the intention of compelling X to perform a certain act and/or to intimidate her by:
> — telephoning X repeatedly and
> — repeatedly making threats against X, such as 'if you leave me I'll kill you' and 'I'm going to finish you off', or words to that effect and
> — threatening X through her family and workmates and
> — approaching a relative and workmate in a threatening manner (on 9 May 2000) [witness 1], another workmate and on 7 July 2001 [witness 2] X's sister and
> — following X to her place of work and
> — on 28 January, 22 February, 26 February and 9 May 2001, harassing X by loitering near her work and
> — sending X a threatening letter and
> — harassing X by standing and shouting in front of her home on 8 November 2000, 7 January 2001 and 9 May 2001.[28]

Alongside technological and social developments, new legislation also gives rise to questions of interpretation, particularly at the start, and so requires the courts to play a lawmaking role. One of the many examples is article 285b of the Dutch Criminal Code, which entered into force on 12 July 2000. This article makes it a criminal offence to systematically violate another person's personal privacy, in other words to stalk them. A question that arose after the article was introduced concerned the definition of 'systematic'. A case was brought before the Supreme Court in which the defendant had pursued the victim in all the ways listed above for a period of nine months. That this constituted systematic violation of privacy will come as no surprise. In its ruling the Court established a number of criteria regarding the nature,

---

[28] Dutch Supreme Court, 1 June 2004.

duration and frequency of the acts which lower courts could follow in reaching a decision.

VIII. AND THEN THE CURIOUS CASE CONCERNING PEEP SHOWS

The Amsterdam Court of Appeal has concluded that the peep show involves a stage on which a performance is given. Because it can be watched by a number of persons for payment, it amounts to a theatre performance. This is not affected by the erotic nature of the performance, or the fact that it is a continuous performance in which various performers take over from one other, that the length of time the onlookers can watch the performance depends on how much they pay, that each onlooker watches the performance in a more segregated place than is normal in the theatre or that there is no vocal dimension to the performance.[29]

The case cited above was actually about tax law. The Supreme Court decided that peep shows counted as theatre performances and that consequently the lower rate of VAT (6%, as opposed to 19% at the time), applicable to admission to music and theatre performances (operas, operettas, dance, pantomime, revues, musicals, cabaret and lectures) applied. The State Secretary for Finance had lodged an appeal in cassation from this ruling handed down by the court of appeal in Amsterdam. He believed that the appeal court had not taken proper account of the fact that the term 'theatre performance' refers to an interpretation by actors of their roles and is based on a playwright's text and staging. The concept was not to be interpreted as broadly as the appeal court had done. Furthermore, there had to be some kind of cultural dimension comparable with that of a musical or theatre performance, which in the case of a peep show is absent. The Supreme Court took the view that the lower VAT rate applied to admission to peep shows, citing the characteristics listed above. It also concluded that the concept of theatre and musical performance should be broadly interpreted and that the cultural nature or level of a performance was irrelevant. The Court believed that the appeal court's interpretation was correct. This had nothing to do with the personal opinions of the

---

[29] Dutch Supreme Court, 5 December 2008.

Supreme Court justices but was based on the text of the law and the accompanying explanations, where present.

But peep-show organisers could not rejoice for long—before the ruling in this case was handed down, the legislator took action. From 1 January 2008 onwards, the legislation stated that the lower BTW (*Belasting toegevoegde waarde*) rate did not apply to peep shows and other performances whose primary aim was erotic entertainment.

IX. NO ONE HAS THE LAST WORD

As I said in Chapter 1, the three branches of government—the legislature, the executive and the judiciary—keep each other in check in making and implementing laws. The legislature draws the broad lines which the executive puts into practice. Then the courts decide in the individual cases brought before them. This balance also means that the legislature can amend legislation following a court decision, after which the courts may be asked to interpret the new law and to apply it within the limits determined by the Constitution (if constitutional review is allowed) and international law. This is an ongoing process: under the rule of law no one has the last word.

The same dynamic can be seen in the development of the law concerning euthanasia in the Netherlands. The courts were compelled to make decisions in matters where politicians were afraid of getting their fingers burnt. Once developments had been established in a series of judgments, the legislature codified them in law. New, related questions were then put to the courts, and so the process continued. Less dramatic, but still a good example is what happened in the 'peep show case'. After the court had ruled that under existing law a peep show qualified as a theatre performance, the legislature clarified its intentions and amended the legislation.

4

The Judiciary's Relationship with the Constitution and International Law

IN MANY COUNTRIES the Constitution has special status. In some, it takes precedence over other laws. The special status of the Constitution is then often reinforced by the existence of a constitutional court (the German *Bundesverfassungsgericht*, or the *Conseil constitutionnel* in France or the Constitutional Tribunal in Poland for instance), whose task is to ensure that the legislature respects the Constitution. In other countries (like Ireland and Sweden) the Constitution has special status without there being a separate court to uphold it. In this situation, any court or only the highest court may decide whether in enacting laws, the legislature has taken sufficient account of the Constitution.

In the Netherlands the arrangement is very different. Article 120 of the Dutch Constitution states: 'The constitutionality of Acts of Parliament and treaties shall not be reviewed by the courts'. In effect, there is a ban on constitutional review by the courts. If the legislature (government and parliament) adopts legislation, the courts may not give a ruling on whether it is compatible with the Constitution. Nor is there any constitutional court in the Netherlands, unlike in many Western European countries. However, the Dutch courts may review the constitutionality of delegated legislation passed by central government, and regulations adopted by sub-national governments, such as the provincial or municipal authorities.

I. BAN ON CONSTITUTIONAL REVIEW: THE NETHERLANDS AS ODD MAN OUT

It is difficult to explain the prohibition on constitutional review in the Netherlands. It means that the legislature can, with impunity, adopt an Act of Parliament that is in breach of the Constitution and there is nothing the courts can do about it. What is more, if it transpires that existing legislation, either primary or secondary, conflicts with a new constitutional provision, it remains in force until it is amended in line with the Constitution (see article 140 of the Constitution: 'Existing Acts of Parliament and other regulations and decrees which are in conflict with an amendment to the Constitution shall remain in force until provisions are made in accordance with the Constitution'). You might regard article 140 as a guarantee of stability, preventing a situation in which all kinds of rules and regulations suddenly have to change.

Admittedly, it is not the case that an Act of Parliament in the Netherlands is at no point reviewed in light of the Constitution. That review is carried out by the bodies involved in making laws: the Council of State in its advisory role and the legislative branch: government and both houses of parliament. Traditionally, the Senate plays a key role in this process and should continue to do so. It is and will remain first and foremost the responsibility of these bodies—and this is also the case in countries which do have a system of constitutional review—to ensure that no legislation that is in breach of the Constitution reaches the statute book. An example is provided by the Council of State's advice not to introduce a ban on the wearing of the niqab. The Council considered there was insufficient justification for the violation of freedom of religion, protected by article 6 of the Constitution, such a ban would entail.

Though concern for constitutionality is an inherent part of the legislative process, it is still possible, in practice, for the application of a law to come into conflict with a constitutional rule, even in countries where prior constitutional review (ie before the law concerned enters into force) is allowed. As pointed out earlier, the legislator cannot foresee every situation. It would then seem logical for the courts to be able to waive application of the law in question. In the Netherlands this is impossible. This implies a failure to take seriously the important position the Constitution should occupy in the Dutch polity.

II. EFFECT OF INTERNATIONAL LAW: LILIAN JANSE, SGP LOCAL COUNCIL MEMBER

The way international law is implemented in national systems varies according to country. States make agreements with each other that impose certain obligations on their signatories, for example to recognise certain human rights (human rights conventions). In some countries, the individual can then directly invoke an article of such a convention, for instance one providing for freedom of religion. Legal theorists call this a monist system. In other countries that article must first be transposed into national law—the dualist system.

States may also agree with each other that they will take certain measures to reduce CO_2 emissions (as agreed in the Paris Agreement on climate change at the end of 2015), establish border controls or set up an international patent court. Such matters do not in principle lend themselves to direct invocation by individual citizens.

'Supreme Court: SGP (Dutch Calvinist Party) no longer permitted to exclude women' was the headline in a Dutch magazine in 2010. Four years later, a television news channel announced 'Historic moment in Vlissingen: female SGP member elected to local council'. Neither of these news items would have appeared without the Supreme Court ruling quoted below, which illustrates the effect of international law in national legal orders.

> In our system, as in many other democratic electoral systems, political parties play a central role in the election of the members of publicly elected bodies (general representative bodies in the words of article 4 of the Constitution). This is because a person's exercise of his/her right to stand for election is dependent on his/her nomination as candidate by a political party, which in turn is dependent on membership of that party. [...]
>
> Under the Convention on the Elimination of All Forms of Discrimination against Women [...], the State has the duty to ensure that political parties not only admit women as members [...] but also allow them to stand as candidates. It follows from this that the SGP's violation of women's fundamental right under the Constitution and the treaties referred to above to stand for election is not justified by the claim that its views with regard to the vocation and position of women in society are rooted in its religious convictions. It is true that the SGP is free to hold these views, that the civil courts are not even competent to give an opinion on the extent to which they are important elements in the faith of SGP members, and that the democratic legal order demands tolerance with regard to views rooted in religious or ethical convictions. Nevertheless, none of these considerations prevent the court from concluding that the way in which the SGP puts its views into practice when it comes to nominating candidates for general representative bodies is unacceptable.[1]

---

[1] Dutch Supreme Court, 9 April 2010.

On 19 March 2014 Lilian Janse was elected to the local council in Vlissingen. This may not seem in any way remarkable. But it was the first time since the founding of the SGP, an orthodox Protestant party, that a woman member was nominated as candidate to a representative body. And this event was preceded by a long battle that had gone all the way up to the Supreme Court. The SGP believed that women should not sit on representative bodies, including local councils. In their view, men and women are of equal value, as God's creatures, but God did not create them equal. In God's order the man has authority over the woman and governance is reserved to men. Women are therefore permitted to vote but they may not stand for election.

In line with these views, the SGP did not nominate women candidates for election. A number of organisations, including the Dutch section of the International Commission of Jurists, challenged the SGP and the State, citing the Convention on the Elimination of All Forms of Discrimination against Women which, as its name implies, prohibits sexual discrimination. In fact article 7 states explicitly that women should be eligible for election to all publicly elected bodies.

The issue was raised by a number of women's and human rights organisations, first before The Hague District Court, then The Hague Court of Appeal and lastly the Supreme Court. Initially the lawsuit was against the State alone. At the appeal stage the SGP joined the proceedings. The State was accused of allowing a political party to exclude women from the right to stand for election. The plaintiffs were successful before all three courts. The Supreme Court held that the prohibition on discrimination weighed more heavily than freedom of religion and freedom of association (invoked by both the State and the SGP). The case is incidentally also a good illustration of the role of courts in practice when fundamental rights clash, but I will return to this point later.

After the Supreme Court handed down its ruling some discussion ensued on its execution. The SGP also took the case to the European Court of Human Rights, claiming that the judgment had violated its freedom of religion and association. Its application was however unsuccessful. The ECtHR found that the Supreme Court had been correct to conclude that the SGP's position was unacceptable, regardless of the deeply held religious convictions on which it was based.[2]

---

[2] ECtHR, 10 July 2012, no 58369/10 (Decision on admissibility in *Staatkundig Gereformeerde Partij v the Netherlands*).

It took four years before the ruling was put into practice, in the municipal elections in Vlissingen. No male candidates put themselves forward to lead the party in the local council but there was one female candidate, Lilian Janse, who was subsequently elected. And there the matter would seem to have ended. The case illustrates the very significant influence of international law in the Netherlands and the role played by the courts.

Although, as explained above, constitutional review by the courts is not permitted in the Netherlands, the country does go further than many Western European nations with regard to review in light of treaties and of resolutions passed by international organisations. In fact, the Dutch Constitution is an exception in this sense.

Article 93 of the Dutch Constitution.

Provisions of treaties and of resolutions by international institutions which may be binding on all persons by virtue of their contents shall become binding after they have been published.

Article 94.

Statutory regulations in force within the Kingdom shall not be applicable if such application is in conflict with provisions of treaties or of resolutions by international institutions that are binding on all persons.

So Dutch citizens can invoke treaty law (as happened in the SGP case with the Convention on the Elimination of All Forms of Discrimination against Women), and national legislation that is incompatible with treaty law is then inapplicable (as in the case of the little boy Charles F. discussed below).

Individuals can apply to the courts for a decision on whether article 94 of the Constitution applies to a particular situation. And if application of national legislation would clash with a universally binding provision of a treaty or resolution of an international organisation, the latter takes precedence. In this way, the Dutch courts act in practice as a constitutional court. The result is a system that in its essence is little different from that in countries in which review of national laws in light of nationally guaranteed fundamental rights, enshrined in a constitution, is permitted.

To sum up, the Dutch courts may not review the applicability of the law in light of the Constitution, but must (in most cases) review it in light of treaties. In the current context, where many fundamental rights are protected by treaties, this leads to a strange situation. The courts can offer no protection against legislation that breaches the fundamental rights laid down in the Constitution. Only if such rights are also contained in a binding international instrument can the courts review the law in question. In the field of human rights, therefore, the Dutch Constitution is relatively dormant; this undermines its authority and does not promote a serious constitutional debate. It means that discussions on human rights, even if they are enshrined in the Constitution, are discussed in court on the basis of the treaty provisions in which they are formulated, usually in the European Convention on Human Rights. One advantage of allowing constitutional review would be that when the courts place limits on certain human rights, it would no longer be 'Europe's fault' but the fault of the Netherlands' own Constitution. Which might in turn improve acceptance of the European Court of Human Rights.

My experience has taught me that constitutional review is a good idea. It contributes to giving the national constitution a more central place than other laws. Especially nowadays, when nationalist sentiment is on the rise, it can reduce the gap between the people and constitutional values. But this is subject to two conditions. First judges have to exercise restraint. As I argued earlier, they must not overplay their hand and must refrain, except where it is impossible, from interfering in choices that should be made by government and legislature. This does not mean that when confronted with clear violations of the constitution they must keep silent. But political choices that do not infringe constitutional values have to be respected. Second, the nomination of judges must not be based on their political preferences. The independence of the judiciary must not be put at risk by political nominations. I realise that this standpoint runs counter to nomination practice in the US Supreme Court and to a lesser extent in the German *Bundesverfassungsgericht*. But I believe those practices do not fully respect the great value of judicial independence.

III. PRECEDENCE OF INTERNATIONAL LAW:
THE CASE OF CHARLES F

Article 8, paragraph 1 of the ECHR implies that a man and his biological child with whom he has established family life within the meaning of this provision are in principle entitled to have their relationship legally recognised as a family-law relationship. This means that on the basis of a system such as that laid down in article 1:221 and 222 of the Civil Code, such a father cannot be denied the option of acknowledging paternity of the child. [...]

Pending the introduction of new legislation it must be assumed [...] that in any event the provision of the Convention referred to above cannot be reconciled with a situation in which the possibility of acknowledging paternity is restricted by a right of veto vested in the mother which is not open to review by a court. A reasonable interpretation of the current legislation, taking account of article 8 ECHR, therefore means that even if the mother refuses the necessary consent, a legally valid acknowledgment of paternity can be achieved through the avenue referred to in 3.2, provided the refusal of consent can only be interpreted as abuse of the consent requirement laid down in article 1:224, paragraph 1, opening words and (d).[3]

This case concerned a man and a woman who had had a relationship which lasted around two years. On 20 July 1984, a child, named Charles, was born. Shortly afterwards, the relationship ended. The man remained involved in the care and upbringing of the child.[4] Charles was later placed under a supervision order and, together with the woman's two children by another man, was placed in a foster family. The man had wanted to acknowledge paternity of the child immediately after his birth, but Charles' mother refused to give consent, claiming that the man was not the biological father. According to article 1:224 of the old Civil Code, her consent was required for an acknowledgment of paternity. The man took the matter to court and his suit was finally successful before the Supreme Court. The Court gave precedence to a provision of international law which could not be reconciled with a mother having a right of veto that could not be reviewed by a court. Inspired by the ECHR, the Supreme Court held that the Dutch legislation allowed for a mother's refusal to cooperate in such circumstances to be deemed an abuse of rights. This is known as a treaty-compliant interpretation: the legislation is interpreted in such a way that it does not conflict with treaty law. This also makes it unnecessary to waive application of that legislation as required by article 94 of the Constitution.

---

[3] Dutch Supreme Court, 8 April 1988.
[4] Amsterdam Appeal Court, 10 October 1988.

IV. JUDICIAL RESTRAINT: LEGISLATOR AND JUDGE,
EACH IN THEIR OWN DOMAIN

This system of precedence sometimes gives rise to problems. If there are a variety of ways to solve the conflict, judges often exercise restraint. After all, it is not up to the judiciary to make political choices.

To illustrate: Titia Beukema was the mother of twins, Josje and Sander. The twins' father was a man named Wouter van Veen. The couple were not married. Wouter had not wanted to acknowledge paternity of the twins because under the old article 1:5 of the Dutch Civil Code they would then bear their father's surname, which was apparently not what the couple wanted. They faced a choice between two evils: acknowledgment and registration of the father's surname, or no acknowledgment and the children would bear their mother's surname. The official at the Register of Births, Deaths and Marriages refused to adopt a third possibility: stating in the birth certificate that Van Veen was the father but did not wish to acknowledge paternity. The parents invoked article 26 of the International Covenant on Civil and Political Rights, which contains a general prohibition of discrimination.

> All persons are equal before the law and are entitled without any discrimination to the equal protection of the law. In this respect, the law shall prohibit any discrimination and guarantee to all persons equal and effective protection against discrimination on any ground such as race, colour, sex, language, religion, political or other opinion, national or social origin, property, birth or other status.

According to the Supreme Court, the Dutch legislation on naming children born outside wedlock was in breach of this provision.[5] The problem was that this could be resolved in a number of ways. One would be to give parents the right to choose a surname once the father had acknowledged paternity, or, if no joint choice was made, to give the child the mother's or the father's surname. Or the child could bear both surnames, though this might lead to conflict as to which surname would come first. In other words, a range of options was available. In the Supreme Court's view, deciding between them fell outside the courts' lawmaking powers. That is an elegant way of saying that the Supreme Court does not wish to step into the legislator's shoes.

---

[5] Dutch Supreme Court, 23 September 1988.

The Court thus established that there was a conflict but referred the matter to the legislature.

The Supreme Court dealt in more detail with the different tasks of the three branches of government in a tax case dating from 12 May 1999.

In this kind of situation, bearing in mind the nature of the area of law at issue, two interests have to be weighed against each other. The advantage of the Court itself remedying this insufficiency in the legislation is that it can immediately offer the interested party effective protection; the disadvantage is that in our constitutional relations the courts must exercise restraint in intervening in this way with regard to a statutory provision. [...] This weighing of interests will generally lead to the court immediately remedying the insufficiency if Dutch legislation, the cases it regulates and the principles on which it is based, or the parliamentary history of an Act of Parliament make it sufficiently clear how this should be done. However, in cases where a number of solutions are conceivable and the choice among them is partly dependent on general government policy considerations, or if major choices of a legal and political nature have to be made, it is appropriate for the courts to leave that choice to the legislature, in connection both with the constitutionally desirable judicial restraint referred to in 3.14, and the courts' restricted options in this area. However, it cannot be ruled out that the weighing of interests will have a different outcome if the legislature is aware that a particular statutory provision gives rise to unjustified discrimination within the meaning of the treaty provision referred to above, but has failed to introduce a provision which would remove the discrimination in question.

This ruling referred to the restraint to be exercised by the courts. This goes to the heart of good relations between legislature and judiciary, as I pointed out in Chapter 3 on the subject of the democracy principle. In essence, when an important question regarding the organisation and shaping of state and society is at issue, the necessary choices must be made by the legislature. This is not, after all, the task of the courts. And so it is up to the legislature to decide whether children whose paternity has been judicially acknowledged should bear their mother's surname, their father's, or both, or whether other choices should be made. Yet in the tax case the Supreme Court sounded a note of warning. If the legislature did not resolve the issue within a reasonable time, the Court would give a decision. This must mean that it was assuming a conflict between the application of national law and treaty law. If there were no conflict, the courts would not be competent—under the Netherlands' constitutional arrangements—to take action and such a warning would be inappropriate.

It emerges from the above that the Supreme Court acts with restraint. It does not seize on every conflict between the application of national or treaty law to resolve the situation itself. The Court holds back, and that has to do with a specific view of the relationship between judiciary and legislator.

Following a ruling from a national court on national law, the legislature can amend the law. This is illustrated by the case regarding the fees to be paid for an identity card.[6]

Because amending a treaty or convention is much more difficult than amending legislation, the courts must exercise even more care and restraint in interpreting a treaty. Otherwise the balance of power could be disturbed. Restraint is thus particularly called for where the courts apply international law.

V. CONFLICT BETWEEN FUNDAMENTAL RIGHTS: THIEVES AND PAEDOPHILES

The importance of the courts' duty to guarantee respect for the fundamental rights enshrined in treaties—even when this goes against popular opinion—is equalled only by the complexity and sensitivity of the considerations this entails. Above all, when fundamental rights conflict. A good example in the Netherlands is that of Leen van Dijke, at the time a member of parliament, who on the basis of his religious convictions was reported to have equated practising homosexuals with thieves with regard to the sinfulness of their conduct.

In an interview published in a Dutch weekly magazine, Van Dijke was alleged to have said, 'Yes, why should a practising homosexual be any better than a thief?'. The appeal court acquitted him on a charge of insulting behaviour. In its judgment, the appeal court held that freedom

---

[6] In a ruling of 9 September 2011 the tax division of the Supreme Court held that there was no sound legal basis for the fees levied by local authorities for issuing identity cards. On 21 September in that same year the competent Minister introduced a Bill to remedy this situation that was approved by the House of Representatives on 29 September, agreed by the Senate on 11 October and published on 14 October 2011.

of religion and of expression can play a role in determining whether a statement—in itself offensive or hurtful—is also insulting. It further held that the comparison of homosexual practices with other acts that were also sinful in terms of Van Dijke's religious beliefs had remained within the limits of what is acceptable and was therefore not insulting. The Supreme Court upheld this judgment. It took into account the fact that the statements in question were obviously a direct expression of Van Dijke's religious beliefs and as such were important to him in the context of public debate.

In this case protecting freedom of religion and expression entailed offending the gay community. They might have regarded this as discriminatory. The ban on discrimination is an important aspect of the rule of law. At the same time, freedom of religion and expression are equally important values under the rule of law. And in the context of his views, Van Dijke belonged to a minority, just as homosexuals do. It will be clear that the courts were confronted with a difficult choice.[7]

Another example is provided by a case in which the civil division of the Supreme Court decided that the Martijn association (which advocated social acceptance of paedophilia) should be banned and disbanded because its activities were contrary to public policy.[8] That was not as straightforward a decision as it might appear. Two important constitutional rights were at issue here: freedom of expression (article 7 of the Dutch Constitution) and freedom of association (article 8). Generally speaking, great restraint must be exercised when considering the banning and dissolution of an association. But in this highly exceptional case the Supreme Court held that this was necessary in the interests of protecting the health, rights and freedom of children. The Supreme Court had to base its opinion on the facts established by the appeal court, namely that the association trivialised the dangers of sexual contact with children, in fact glamourised such contacts and actively propagated its views. However, in the Netherlands the prevailing view of sexual contact between adults and young children is that it is a genuine and serious assault on the physical and sexual integrity of the child that can lead to substantial and long-lasting psychological

---

[7] Dutch Supreme Court, 9 January 2001.
[8] Dutch Supreme Court, 18 April 2014.

damage. Children in fact require protection from adults who indulge in such activities, since their youth and vulnerability put them in a position of dependence.

VI. UNDEMOCRATIC POLITICAL PARTIES: TOLERATING THE INTOLERANT?

Fundamental rights such as freedom of association and the right to stand as a candidate in elections can sometimes endanger other democratic values. I am not referring here to violent opposition to democracy. The criminal law has instruments to tackle this problem. Every country has laws that criminalise causing violent disorder. The more important issue is how we can tackle people and parties that are a threat to democracy in a non-violent way. I believe they must be opposed because we have to defend non-negotiable values.[9] How can this be done? There is a formal instrument and there are informal strategies. The formal instrument enables us to ban political parties that do not subscribe to democratic values. This is possible in several countries, including Poland and the Netherlands. Where this is so, the judiciary plays a key role. Article 2:20 of the Dutch Civil Code states that a legal person whose activities are contrary to public order can on the application of the public prosecutor be banned and dissolved by the courts. In the parliamentary debate on this provision it was made clear that the article refers to activities that undermine the foundations of our legal system, such as violence or the threat of violence, racial discrimination, inciting hatred or pleading impunity for those who kill certain groups of people.[10]

In the Netherlands there are three examples of parties that were banned on such grounds. In 1998, Amsterdam district court ruled that an extreme right-wing party should be banned and dissolved.[11]

The aim of this political party was to incite or propagate discrimination against foreigners. According to the court this was contrary to public order as referred to in article 2:20 of the Civil Code. In 2015 the

---

[9] Ian Buruma, *Murder in Amsterdam* (Atlantic Books 2006) p 29.
[10] Gelijn Molier, 'Het verbod van een politieke partij' (Banning a political party), *Nederlands Juristenblad* 2016, p 2438–2446, p 2442.
[11] Amsterdam district court, 18 November 1998.

government published a memorandum on anti-democratic organisations in which it stated that in order to ban political parties there had to be an imminent danger their anti-democratic political goals would be achieved.[12] This means that simply proclaiming such goals is not sufficient for a banning order.

On the one hand, this approach leaves room for political opponents to be heard in the country's political assemblies, thus contributing to democratic debate. Radical voices must be heard. Other political parties must take account of those voices in order to create a state in which minorities feel they belong. On the other hand, there must be an instrument to ban such groups when there is imminent danger they will undermine the values of democracies governed by the rule of law.

The European Court of Human Rights was confronted with this problem in several cases. In the case of the *Socialist Party v Turkey*, the Court held that 'It is of the essence of democracy to allow diverse political programmes to be proposed and debated, even those that call into question the way a state is currently organised, provided that they do not harm democracy itself'.[13] This implies that the Court considers it acceptable that a national state takes action against parties that will undermine democracy itself. The Refah case is also relevant in this respect.[14] Refah was an Islamic party in Turkey. It was also the largest political party: it was expected to win as much as 67% of the vote in upcoming elections. The Turkish Constitutional Court had dissolved Refah on the grounds that it had become a centre of activities contrary to the principle of secularism, enshrined in the Turkish Constitution. Refah applied to the European Court of Human Rights, basing its complaint on article 11 of the Convention, which guarantees freedom of association. The Court held:

> ... that a political party may promote a change in the law or the legal and constitutional structures of the State on two conditions: firstly, the means used to that end must be legal and democratic; secondly, the change proposed must itself be compatible with fundamental democratic principles. It necessarily follows that a political party whose leaders incite to violence or

---

[12] Parliamentary Papers, 2014/2015, 29279, 226.
[13] ECtHR 25 May 1998, 20/1997/804/1007.
[14] ECtHR 13 February 1998, 41340/98.

put forward a policy which fails to respect democracy or which is aimed at the destruction of democracy and the flouting of the rights and freedoms recognised in a democracy cannot lay claim to the Convention's protection against penalties imposed on those grounds.

According to the ECtHR the Turkish Constitutional Court had not violated the Convention in banning the Refah party.

In this judgment, which is in line with other decisions, it is clear that the European Court of Human Rights drew certain lines that have to be respected with regard to political parties that do not subscribe to the principles of the rule of law. It does not prohibit a relationship between state and religion. But some distance between state and religion has to be maintained in order to respect the rights of those who do not subscribe to the mainstream belief, or who are agnostic or atheist.

5

The Relationship between the Judiciary and the Executive

I N NOVEMBER 2016, the High Court in the UK ruled that it was Parliament—and not the Prime Minister, using prerogative powers—that had the legal authority to trigger article 50 of the Treaty on the European Union and thus begin the UK's exit from the EU. The Daily Mail published the pictures of the three judges involved, over the headline 'Enemies of the people'. In this case, the judiciary intervened with regard to the competences of the legislative and the executive branches of government. In a way you might say that the High Court judges emphasised the importance of the standpoint of the representatives of the people alongside that of the executive. On 24 January the judgment of the High Court was upheld by the Supreme Court.

Members of the executive sometimes wonder if effective government is still possible with all the rules and regulations that nowadays encumber it. In the Netherlands, for example, endless proceedings delayed the construction of the double-track freight railway from the port of Rotterdam to Germany, known as the Betuwe Line. The protection of endangered species sometimes takes precedence over building plans. Headlines such as 'Vole wins the battle', 'Spiny loach halts work on new rail connection' or 'Hamster defeats plans to build business park' are common in a number of European countries. 'Enough is enough' is the reaction of many a frustrated public servant. Indeed, towards the end of the 1990s, the Dutch government went so far as to set up a committee, chaired by a former minister, that criticised the legal obstacles encountered by the public authorities. The judiciary is of course familiar with these views. In proceedings where the executive fears excessive interference by the courts, it constantly reiterates themes such as 'executive power' and 'freedom to act'. The opposing party naturally asks the court to consider its needs and entitlements, for example, the right to peaceful enjoyment of its property. It is precisely the task of the judiciary to determine whether in specific cases the public interest must take precedence over the protection of individual citizens. An individual may be confronted with plans to build on the meadow opposite his house, or a reduction in the value of his property because of motorway construction in the vicinity, or environmental damage caused by public works which breaches the regulations. He may thus come into conflict with a local or national authority charged with economic development. In such cases the courts have to weigh all the interests involved, just as they do in disputes between private individuals and businesses, and therefore take account of each side's interests. And they do this not on the basis of a whim but of rules of law laid down by the legislature. And these include rules protecting endangered species.

I. REVIEW BY THE COURTS: FLORISTS AND VOLES

Guldemond, a florist in the Dutch village of Lisse had owned various parcels of land in neighbouring Noordwijkerhout since 1905. On his own land he dug a twelve-metre wide drainage channel, which he used for many years without any problem. The channel intersected with a footpath. In 1914, the Noordwijkerhout local authority started preparations to fill the channel so that the footpath could be used again. Guldemond opposed this plan and filed interim injunction proceedings before the civil court, demanding that the authority bring a halt to the work and seeking permission to remove the sand that had already been dumped in the channel. Noordwijkerhout argued that the civil courts had no jurisdiction, because its actions in the matter fell under public law: section 179h of the Municipalities Act as it read at the time stated that local authorities were responsible for ensuring that public highways could be used by the public. Both The Hague District Court and the Court of Appeal declared themselves competent, as civil courts, because the dispute concerned a civil-law matter. The Supreme Court agreed, ruling that under section 2 of the 1827 Judiciary (Organisation) Act the jurisdiction of the court is dependent on the right for which the person concerned seeks protection. In this case, a classic civil right was at issue—Guldemond's property rights.[1]

---

[1] Dutch Supreme Court, 31 December 1915.

That the courts also afford citizens protection from government was established by this ruling. Early in the nineteenth century the government had tried to sideline the courts in cases against public authorities, claiming that they had no jurisdiction unless the monarch decided otherwise. Quite rightly, there was strong resistance to this idea in the House of Representatives. In the case of *Guldemond v Noordwijkerhout* this question was put to the Supreme Court. According to the Court, the 1815 Constitution aimed to limit the powers of the 'Administration' (ie government) and to put property rights 'unconditionally under the protection of the courts'. This was a major achievement: the courts thus acquired a new task, that of scrutinising—to a certain extent— the actions of the executive. So the executive can be brought to heel. And perhaps more important, the executive is aware of this and has to anticipate the response of the courts in making decisions.

As I said above, this ruling makes it clear that citizens can count on the courts' protection from the executive. Below we will see that in the course of the twentieth century this protection was consolidated through the doctrine of tort (or wrongful acts) by the State and the establishment of separate administrative courts. Later on, even the criminal courts began to play a role in offering protection from government.

II. TORT BY THE STATE: A BUTTER MERCHANT AND AYAAN HIRSI ALI

Ostermann sold butter and margarine in Amsterdam and wanted to export a consignment of his wares. He needed a permit to do so. The customs officials refused to complete the necessary formalities. Ostermann took the position that they were legally obliged to do so. He therefore filed a suit against the State, claiming damages. The district and appeal courts in Amsterdam ruled against him: though the officials had probably failed to meet their obligations under public law, a citizen could derive no rights from this breach. In 1924 the Supreme Court overturned these rulings. It held that the authorities must meet their obligations under the law. If they do not, and fail to respect statutory provisions of whatever nature, they have committed a tort and must pay damages.[2]

---

[2] Dutch Supreme Court, 20 November 1924.

In the interests of providing a secure residence for Ayaan Hirsi Ali, at the time a member of parliament with outspoken views on Islam, the government bought an apartment in a complex in The Hague and put stringent security arrangements in place. The other residents of the complex suffered nuisance as a result and filed interim injunction proceedings. This action failed, but on appeal they were successful. The State then lodged an appeal in cassation before the Supreme Court. The Court overturned the appeal court's ruling, so the residents lost their case.

> The State has a margin of decision and policy-making discretion with regard to the seriousness of the threat and the use of the high-security apartment. When the courts assess the gravity of the risks posed by the threat and in that connection the need to use the high-security apartment in that specific location, as well as the feasibility, necessity and effectiveness of the security arrangements made, it will have to examine whether the State could reasonably have come to the conclusion that the threat on the one hand and the security arrangements on the other were of such a nature that the use of the high-security apartment was a responsible measure in light of the risks for other residents.[3]

The Ostermann ruling made it clear that public authorities cannot get away with wrongful acts. This may seem obvious, nowadays, but was for a long period anything but. The doctrine of tort by the State was shaped in a long series of Supreme Court decisions, preceded and followed by commentary by legal theorists and practicing lawyers. It is now possible to say that government can be held responsible for every tort it commits and that everyone affected by such an act can in principle mount a successful challenge, seeking damages or an injunction ordering the authorities to desist from the act in question.

In this process, the courts take account of the executive's position. Often enough, they allow the authorities more scope than individuals. The reason for this is that government must serve the public interest, and that sometimes weighs heavier than an individual's interests. That was the case in the controversial proceedings concerning Ayaan Hirsi Ali's high-security home. There the Supreme Court referred specifically to the executive's decision and policy-making discretion. In other words, the courts will not replace the authorities' view of a matter

---

[3] Dutch Supreme Court, 20 October 2006.

with their own. On the contrary, their role is to examine whether the authorities have exercised their powers reasonably.

III. PROTECTION UNDER ADMINISTRATIVE LAW: BUSINESS SUCCESSION AND A BERTH ON THE APELDOORN CANAL

A man dies, leaving a wife and two children. They are aware that if you have a business, the first million or so euros is exempt from inheritance tax, as is 83% of the remainder. Which makes quite a difference. Normally, there is an exemption of around €20,000 and inheritance tax is payable at 10% on the first €120,000 and 20% on the remaining amount. But there was no business involved in this particular case, so the heirs could not benefit from the large exemption available to entrepreneurs. They invoked the principle of equal treatment. Neither the district court nor the Supreme Court agreed. The latter held that there were sound, objective reasons for treating business assets differently from private assets: it is important to ensure that the levying of inheritance tax does not pose a threat to the continuity of the business. If the amount of inheritance tax to be paid is too high, a small family business, for example, can end up with serious liquidity problems.[4]

It has long been possible to challenge the decisions of the tax authorities and social security agencies. The case cited above involved a tax assessment and the plaintiff was only one of thousands of heirs who filed a similar suit. It is a good thing that this is possible: the sums involved, for both individuals and businesses, are often substantial. Think for instance of income tax, which frequently amounts to a third or more of your income. And the State demands its share too in the case of inheritance, and profits made by an enterprise. Home owners pay property tax, calculated on the basis of the value of their houses. This is liable to fluctuate; the calculations involved are not a precise mathematical operation. If you disagree with a decision made by the tax authorities you first have to lodge an objection with the tax administration itself. If you disagree with its decision on your objection, you can apply to the district court for review. After that, appeal to one of the four appeal courts, and finally, appeal in cassation to the Supreme Court are the options.

---

[4] Dutch Supreme Court, 22 November 2013.

As I said earlier, it is possible to challenge decisions made by social security agencies. For example, you are not receiving social assistance benefit but feel you are entitled to it. Or your benefit has been stopped because the agency in question believes you have failed to inform them that you are cohabiting. Or a fine may have been imposed on the grounds of fraud. In all these situations and many others you can lodge an objection with the benefits agency. As in tax cases, you may then apply to the district court, appeal court and sometimes the Supreme Court.

> The owner of a motor boat wanted to moor his boat in Hattem on the Apeldoorn canal. From there it would be easy to supervise his son's repair work on the boat. He applied to the Minister of Infrastructure and the Environment for an exemption from the prohibition on mooring in force at that spot. His application was refused. Following correct procedure, he first lodged an objection to this refusal with the Minister, who declared his objection unfounded. His application for review to the district court was equally unsuccessful. Being a persistent man, he appealed to the Administrative Jurisdiction Division of the Council of State, which upheld the district court's judgment. So his boat never came to be moored on the Apeldoorn canal.[5]

For many years it has been possible in the Netherlands and in other western countries to contest many other decisions emanating from the executive. In the Netherlands this is laid down in the General Administrative Law Act, which established the following procedure. First, an objection can be lodged against any administrative decision with the body that issued the decision. Then, if the objector disagrees with the decision on the objection, he/she can apply to the administrative law sector of the district court for review. Once the district court has decided, appeal lies open to the Administrative Jurisdiction Division of the Council of State, which is the highest court in general administrative matters. As is clear, our boat owner made use of all these options.

IV. REVIEW BY THE CRIMINAL COURTS:
A CANNABIS FARM

On 11 March 2009 the Dutch police raided a house in the village of Blerick with the intention of closing down a cannabis farm at that

---

[5] Administrative Jurisdiction Division, Council of State, 27 August 2014.

address. As we saw in Chapter 1, the inviolability of the home is a fundamental right. A private residence may only be entered under strict conditions. If the occupant refuses entry, under Dutch law authorisation is required from, at the very least, an assistant public prosecutor, a higher-ranking police officer. In this case authorisation was issued by a chief inspector, but it later transpired that he had not passed the examination for assistant public prosecutor and was therefore not qualified to grant authorisation. A single judge trying criminal cases convicted the defendant. He lodged an appeal, claiming that the evidence had been obtained in an unlawful manner, ie on the basis of an invalid authorisation, and that he should therefore be acquitted. And this is what happened. But the case prompted the Supreme Court to give a decision in principle on the consequences of the wrongful acts that took place in the course of this investigation. The Court held that such acts should not automatically lead to the irreversible failure of the prosecution. It developed a refined system under which it is possible to refrain from acquitting a defendant if due process has not been damaged by the wrongful act or if there is another appropriate way of dealing with the situation, such as a reduced sentence.[6]

In many cases, including the one above, the criminal courts in the western world may become involved. They have to decide whether an individual, a company or a local authority (if criminal liability of corporations is renown in the specific country) may be penalised. This entails establishing that they have committed the offence with which they are charged and if they are criminally liable. The first requirement is of course evidence, followed by an assessment of whether the defendant can rely on self-defence, necessity or other grounds for immunity. Other issues that may arise include whether the police, another investigative agency or the public prosecutor have kept to the rules of evidence gathering. The court has thus to decide on their actions. This is not normally the key aspect of the case but can become so. Was it permissible for the police to enter the house? Were there proper grounds for intercepting communications? Was authorisation sought for the use of a criminal to infiltrate an organisation? In such cases the criminal courts, whose primary task is to examine the actions of the defendant and then, possibly, to impose a sentence on him/her, also have to examine the conduct of government.

---

[6] Dutch Supreme Court, 19 February 2013.

In the Netherlands, this is a role the criminal courts only started to play in the second half of the twentieth century, inspired by the case law of the US courts. The criminal courts review the actions of police and the Public Prosecution Service (the public prosecutors) in light of national law, international treaties (in particular the European Convention on Human Rights) and the principles of proper criminal procedure. This type of review may involve a fundamental rule that touches directly on the essence of a fair trial or of what is seen in a state under the rule of law as proper conduct by government.

The legal consequences to be attached to procedural errors by the criminal courts were not, on the whole, regulated by national or treaty law. They were developed through case law. One sanction introduced by the criminal courts was to declare the Public Prosecution Service's application inadmissible, halting the prosecution. Another was to exclude evidence. In such cases evidence obtained as a result of a procedural error, like the unlawful discovery of a cannabis farm in the example above, may not be used to obtain a conviction. If such evidence is decisive to the case, the defendant will be acquitted. These new avenues for the defence were greeted with great enthusiasm by lawyers and led to the failure of many a prosecution.[7] The problem also arose in cases involving administrative fines.

Initially, the criminal courts were fairly inflexible in attaching legal consequences to procedural errors in light of treaty law. Many rulings contained no detailed explanation of the decision. Breaches of the right to be tried within a reasonable time, guaranteed by international instruments like the ECHR, consistently led to the prosecution being barred. It seemed that unlawful evidence gathering must always result in the exclusion of that evidence. In the course of the 1980s the work of the criminal courts came under increased scrutiny and as a result faced growing criticism. Why should a defendant go free simply because the prosecuting authorities had made a mistake? Did that make his crime any less serious? Obviously, irregularities and the overrunning of time limits come in all shapes and sizes: their nature and gravity can be very different depending on the individual case.

---

[7] A J A van Dorst, *Vervolgingsbeletselen* (Impediments to prosecution—in Dutch), Zwolle, Tjeenk Willink, 1989, p V.

If this is insufficiently appreciated, the relationship between error and legal consequences can easily become disproportionate. The inflexible application of radical responses to procedural errors soon gave rise to concern, and it became clear that here too a weighing of interests was necessary in each individual case.

Towards the end of the eighties the courts began to take a less radical approach. A breach of the reasonable time requirement no longer led automatically to the prosecution being barred; instead it could be settled through a reduction in sentence. A significantly higher standard for barring prosecution due to unlawful investigation was developed.

But in the meantime, the general public had gained the impression that the criminal courts were constantly letting defendants get away scot-free because of trivial errors. An over-simplified view of course, but looking back, not entirely without substance.[8] Public dissatisfaction regarding the way the criminal law system operated was an important catalyst for the Procedural Errors Act, passed in the mid-nineties. The principal aim of the Act is to address the need for differentiation by the courts in determining the legal consequences of procedural errors. Because of the huge variety of possible defects, it is not feasible to establish specific consequences for each breach of the rules and would create far too rigid a system. A weighing of interests is necessary in individual cases. The criminal courts are in far better a position than the legislator to assess the interests involved. Unlike the legislator, the courts can take account of all the circumstances of the case. From this perspective, the legislature confirmed the central position the criminal courts had established for themselves in determining the legal consequences of procedural errors. It provided for three options in article 359a of the Code of Criminal Procedure: barring prosecution, excluding evidence and reducing sentences (another example of the codification of case law). The legislature also specifically stated that the application of legal consequences disproportionate to the error should in the future be avoided.

As a result of the introduction of this provision, an inflexible, knee-jerk response to procedural errors based on implicit arguments of

---

[8] Y Buruma, *De aandacht van de strafrechter* (The attention of the criminal courts—in Dutch), inaugural address, Nijmegen. Deventer, Gouda Quint, 1996.

principle is now a thing of the past. This is reflected in the Supreme Court's umbrella ruling on article 359a.[9]

Ensuring proper investigation of offences remains of vital importance to the rule of law but other interests may oppose it. For example, the interests of society and the victim in the prosecution process. These too must be taken into account under the rule of law. In the matter of procedural errors, a shift took place in the administration of justice from an approach in which the integrity of the criminal law process demanded that evidence be excluded, regardless of the nature and gravity of the error, to one in which there was scope for weighing the seriousness of the error and the consequences for the defendant. This shift was then explicitly anchored in legislation.[10]

In the law of England and Northern Ireland things developed in a different way. Sometimes there is a statutory time-limit for instituting criminal proceedings. If there is, then proceedings begun after the expiry of that time-limit are invalid (and if by oversight they are commenced out of time and a conviction is imposed, it will be set aside automatically).

Criminal proceedings can be stopped, at the request of the defendant, where they constitute 'abuse of process'. This is a hydra-headed concept, one head of which is where there has been an unreasonable delay in either starting proceedings, or in expediting them once they have been started. But in a leading case[11] the House of Lords decided by a majority that delay amounting to a breach of article 6 does not, on its own, justify putting a stop to the proceedings. To justify a stay for abuse of process, the delay must have caused some real difficulty for the defendant.

V. REVIEW BY THE CRIMINAL COURTS: THE PIKMEER LAKE

The head of the local authority department responsible for new construction work in Boarnsterhim, Friesland, was prosecuted on the charge that

---

[9]   Dutch Supreme Court, 30 March 2004.

[10]   See R Kuiper, *Vormfouten. De juridische consequenties van vormverzuimen in strafzaken* (English summary: *Procedural errors: the legal consequences of breaches of procedural rules in criminal proceedings*), thesis, Nijmegen, Deventer, Kluwer 2014.

[11]   Attorney General's Ref (No 2 of 2001) [2003] UKHL 68, 2004 2 WLR 10.

under his management the authority had dumped polluted sludge in the Pikmeer lake near the village of Grouw. This was a contravention of environmental legislation.

The question was whether a local authority could be held criminally liable. Until then, the assumption had always been that it could not. In a fine and at the same time self-evident consideration, the Supreme Court took as its basic premise that 'like every individual citizen, the public authorities, including both central government and sub-national authorities such as provinces, municipalities and water boards, have to abide by the law'. In itself, this did not mean that the authorities or people who worked for them could be held criminally liable. The Supreme Court concluded that a public authority only falls outside the scope of the criminal law where its activities:

> ... by their nature and having regard to the body of Dutch legislation can, by law, only be carried out by public officials in the framework of the performance of the duties assigned to public bodies, so that the possibility of third parties acting on the same footing as the public body in question is excluded.

This is quite a mouthful, but what it means is that the key question is whether the action at issue is something only the public authorities can perform. Commercial enterprises can also dump sludge of course, but issuing a passport is an activity more naturally reserved to the authorities.[12]

This ruling, known as the Pikmeer II ruling, heralded a new development. The Dutch legislature had not regulated this issue when in the 1970s, as one of the first in Western Europe, it introduced criminal liability for legal persons. It left it to the courts to decide whether the public authorities could also be held criminally liable. For many years the Supreme Court played for time. But in the ruling cited above it concluded that both public and professional opinion had changed. It also referred to a motion in the House of Representatives, adopted unanimously, that there should be more scope for criminal proceedings against public authorities. The Pikmeer II judgment is not only of major importance for the position of the courts in relation to the executive. It is also highly relevant to the relationship with the

---

[12] Dutch Supreme Court, 6 January 1998.

legislature: the Supreme Court explicitly stated that the legislature had not wanted to regulate the matter because 'this is an intractable issue which is difficult to condense in legal provisions and is therefore left to the courts.' The legislature thus authorised the judiciary to resolve a major problem. The reference to public opinion is interesting too, revealing that the Court is not indifferent to prevailing views in society. It was able to take these views into account in this situation because the legislature had allowed it the scope to do so. This is more difficult if the legislature has not made specific provisions in an Act but in the accompanying explanatory memorandum has expressed definite views tending in a particular direction. Incidentally, the new approach heralded by Pikmeer II was not extended to include central government, which still cannot be prosecuted for criminal behaviour.

In the law of England and Wales 'corporations' can be prosecuted for criminal offences. A corporation is what continental lawyers (and increasingly, English lawyers) call legal persons. Whether a public body can be prosecuted or not depends on whether it has 'legal personality' and that depends on the terms of the legislation which created it. Local authorities have legal personality and therefore can, in theory, be prosecuted, though this is very rare. They more usually appear as prosecutors. When the legislator created a new and special offence of corporate manslaughter in the Corporate Manslaughter and Corporate Homicide Act 2007, special provisions were included to list those public bodies which could be prosecuted for the offence.

VI. SHIFT TOWARDS THE EXECUTIVE: A SLIPPERY SLOPE?

The Dutch Authority for the Financial Markets (AFM) imposed an administrative fine on Victor Muller, director and major shareholder of Spyker N.V., a manufacturer of exclusive sports cars. The AFM found that Muller had informed his bank that a major, positive press release about the company was about to be released. This communication did not lead to a transaction, but even in this case, it is prohibited. The bank received more information than any random third party. What is more, sharing such information means it may be passed on to others, who take action on that basis. This is unfair to those who do not have access to the information. In the objection stage (see above under 'Protection under administrative law') the AFM reduced the fine to €24,000, and on review, the district court in Rotterdam reduced it further to €10,000. On appeal, the contravention was confirmed and the amount of the fine set definitively at €11,400.[13]

Until recently, the Netherlands rarely suffered from earth tremors. Unlike the field of law enforcement through the imposition of penalties, where over the last 15 years a real landslide has occurred. By the end of the 1980s, the criminal courts were responsible for imposing most penalties and there was little variation in procedure. Minor offences were dealt with by the sub-district court or a single judge, the rest by full-bench chambers and divisions of the district courts and appeal courts. Tax fines have always been an exception, being imposed by the tax authorities, though more serious tax fraud cases could be heard by the criminal courts. In the late 1980s the police were empowered to issue fines for minor traffic offences, previously the remit of the sub-district courts (since 2002 the limited jurisdiction sector of the district court). Nowadays this sector only enters the picture if an individual applies for review of a decision by the public prosecutor on his objection to the fine imposed. Earlier, the option of what was called a settlement penalty (in lieu of prosecution) had been introduced, with the aim of relieving the burden on the courts.[14]

There is little left of this fairly uncomplicated scenario in the Netherlands and Western Europe. The unending growth in regulation and increasing calls for more enforcement, required a substantial increase in capacity. In the last few decades, demands that the 'lack of enforcement' be addressed became more strident. The shortage certainly had a quantitative element: a greater number of cases had to be disposed of more quickly. But it also had a qualitative aspect: the enforcement of specialist standards (from the amount of nitrate in vegetables, to the stability of ladders) had to be raised to an adequate level. The challenge unleashed extremely creative forces in the legislature.[15]

[13] See AFM statement of 1 May 2012 (https://m.afm.nl/en/nieuws/2012/mei/boete-mededelen-voorwetenschap).

[14] By complying with the conditions imposed by the public prosecutor or the police—usually the payment of a sum of money—the offender could avoid appearing before the court.

[15] G J M Corstens, *Een stille revolutie in het strafrecht* (A quiet revolution in the criminal law—in Dutch) (valedictory address, Nijmegen), Arnhem, Gouda Quint, 1995; H J B Sackers, *Herder, hoeder en handhaver* (Shepherd, guardian and enforcer—in Dutch) (inaugural address, Nijmegen), Arnhem, Roos & Roos, 2010 and A R Hartmann, *Over de grenzen van de dogmatiek en into fuzzy law* (Beyond the limits of dogma into fuzzy law—in Dutch) (inaugural address, Rotterdam), Apeldoorn/Antwerp, Maklu 2011.

The introduction of a penalty order imposed by the Public Prosecution Service and the growth in administrative fines are two of the most essential changes that took place. The new penalty order replaced the settlement penalty referred to above. It is a more radical measure because it gives the Public Prosecution Service a wider range of sanctions to choose from and they can be imposed without recourse to the courts.[16] They may be imposed for minor offences and for serious offences carrying a sentence of up to six years (though the public prosecutor cannot impose custodial sentences). The aim was to achieve a more efficient disposal of cases than was possible with the settlement penalty and traditional criminal proceedings. In the case of administrative fines, over 80 different Acts of Parliament now give the public authorities the power to impose such fines. Administrative authorities like the Dutch Competition Authority perform a supervisory role, but can also fine the persons and companies they supervise. The case of Spyker cited above is only one example. And in the field of competition law, the fines often far exceed what can be imposed under the criminal law.

Both a penalty imposed by the prosecuting authorities and administrative fines can be challenged before the courts. The recipient of such a penalty can lodge an objection with the criminal court. The case will then be decided in open court, thus meeting the requirement of access to an independent and impartial tribunal enshrined in article 6 of the European Convention on Human Rights.[17] If the person concerned does not lodge an objection, the penalty can be enforced. He or she must therefore take the initiative if they wish to lay the matter before

---

[16] The sanctions available include a community service or training order of up to 180 hours, a fine, the withdrawal of confiscated items from circulation, the obligation to pay the State a sum of money for the benefit of the victim, or a ban on driving for up to 6 months. The sanctions may also be imposed by investigating officers, bodies and persons charged with tasks under the public service mandate, and the tax authorities. See too G J M Corstens, *Het Nederlands strafprocesrecht* (Dutch criminal procedure—in Dutch), 8th impression, ed. M J Borgers, Deventer, Kluwer 2014, pp 986–992 and M F Kessler & B F Keulen, *De strafbeschikking* (Penalty imposed by the Public Prosecution Service—in Dutch), Deventer, Kluwer, 2008, pp 20–21 and 109 *ff.*

[17] On p 17 of *De strafbeschikking (ibid)* the authors refer to a number of judgments including ECtHR, 21 February 1984, no 8544/79 (*Özturk v Germany*) and ECtHR, 24 February 1994, no 12547/86 (*Bendenoun v France*).

the courts. The same applies to judicial review of an administrative fine by the administrative courts, though this must be preceded by an objection to the administrative authority that imposed the fine.

A comparable development took place in the UK. First, extensive powers have been given to the police and other enforcement agencies, to issue Fixed Penalty Notices, like the French *amendes forfaitaires*. If you refuse to accept such a notice, you could be prosecuted in the courts (or not, if the enforcement authority decides not to bother). The Crown Prosecution Service has also been given the power to issue 'conditional cautions': you get away with an official warning, instead of a criminal conviction, provided you comply with the condition. But these are relatively uncommon compared with the large number of Fixed Penalty Notices etc.

Secondly, there is an increasing tendency to give administrative authorities the power to impose an 'administrative fine' as an alternative to prosecution. They can be imposed, for example, for late payment of taxes, or by the social security authorities if you continue to claim social security benefits after your person circumstances have changed and you are no longer entitled to them.

In these new models, judicial review is the exception rather than the rule. In a relatively short time, their use has soared and a substantial further rise is to be expected. It may be assumed that they have considerably increased enforcement capacity. That aim has been achieved. But this development also gives rise to questions. Is this transfer of cases away from the courts purely beneficial or have we lost something in the process? Have important judicial functions disappeared under the surface of this churned up landscape? What are the risks?

First, that government loses authority through too much and overly automated enforcement with too little regard for the individual circumstances. Government that is overly concerned with trivialities loses credibility. The Netherlands and other Western European countries have a plethora of rules and regulations. In daily life, a contravention of one of these rules easily occurs. As a result, enforcement tends to kick in increasingly often. Each individual instance may be justified, but at some point one may begin to wonder whether it is wise to seize every single opportunity to impose a sanction.

Second, that because of the wide range of officials with powers to impose sanctions and the multiplicity of enforcement modes, the average citizen no longer sees the wood for the trees. In addition, inequality before the law can arise because the initiative to object to the new sanctions lies with the person penalised and not everybody is equally skilled in finding the right avenues to challenge the sanction, or has the financial means to do so.

Third, that the non-public nature of disposal of cases through a penalty imposed by the prosecuting authorities makes it more difficult to see what is happening in practice. If the person concerned does not challenge the penalty, there is no public scrutiny. The same applies to administrative fines.

Fourth, that reducing the role of the courts, in terms of number of cases, also leads to less judicial scrutiny of what happens in the investigation preceding the imposition of the penalty. If the role of courts shrinks in this way—a process which has admittedly been going on for some time in criminal procedure—the responsibility for scrutiny must be laid elsewhere.

VII. JUDGES MUST BE BRAVE

The courts sometimes hand down decisions that are unwelcome to the executive. Politicians frequently demonstrate a lack of knowledge of the position of the judiciary or how the law stands. To take a Dutch example, the politician who stated that Volkert van der Graaf, convicted of assassinating Pim Fortuyn, leader of a Dutch political party, should not be eligible for release had forgotten that in the Netherlands, prisoners are eligible for release after serving two-thirds of their sentences. Unless of course they have misbehaved in prison. This is laid down in legislation passed by parliament; the courts and the executive have to abide by these rules. On the other hand, judges are independent of the executive. They have to decide on the basis of the law and the knowledge they have acquired regarding the case and the persons concerned. They have not been appointed to please politicians. As the president of the Paris appeal court, Antoine-Jean-Mathieu Seguier said in 1827, after members of government had approached him about a case, 'La Cour rend des arrêts et non pas des services' (the Court renders judgments, not services). No truer word has been spoken. The Hague Court of Appeal and then the Dutch Supreme Court ruled against the State in one of the Srebrenica cases. During the war in the former Yugoslavia in the 1990s, three Muslim men were sent away from the UN compound manned by a Dutch battalion in Srebrenica when it was clear they were in mortal danger. They were subsequently killed by Bosnian-Serb soldiers and paramilitaries. The State was held liable, an unwelcome verdict for the executive. Fortunately, the Dutch prime minister responded appropriately, saying that the judgment would of course be implemented. This might seem obvious, but it exemplifies the proper relationship between the executive and the judiciary. And that is crucial to the rule of law.

6

The Relationship between the Judiciary and Society

THE ADMINISTRATION OF justice is a key element in society. Judges are called upon to settle matters in a wide variety of situations. Issues arising in all sectors of the community end up before the bench. The courts are there to resolve disputes between individual citizens, government, companies and other organisations; where the law has been contravened, their task is to impose penalties on citizens, government, companies or other organisations. The stories below illustrate this point. These are just a few examples from the Dutch media in the second week of September 2014 and the British media in May-June 2016. Every day of the working week, courts decide in these and other cases. All involve dispute settlement and the imposition of penalties, something the judiciary does in 1.7 million cases every year.

I. THE COURTS ARE THERE FOR CITIZENS: MODEL MANDY AND TURBO INVESTMENTS

Jordan Skipp, 23, admitted breaching a non-molestation order made by Oxford Family Court in April this year by approaching and walking alongside Rachel Bisson and trying to communicate with her on May 11 this year. Handed a 12-month conditional discharge and ordered to pay £20 victim surcharge and £85 costs.[1]

Eighteen-year-old Mandy K. from Midden-Delfland has been sentenced to six month's imprisonment, three months of which were suspended, for mugging and possession of a firearm. A former participant in Holland's Next Top Model [the Dutch version of the US television contest] also has

---

[1] Oxford Mail, 10 June 2016.

to undergo treatment for a behavioural disorder and suffers from dimin-
ished responsibility, said the court. On 12 May 2014 Mandy waited for two
13-year-old girls to leave school. The court considered it proven that Mandy,
then still a minor, pushed the girls into an alleyway, took their bank cards
and threatened them with kidnapping and murder. The court suspended
part of the sentence on condition that she undergo treatment in De Waag
[a forensic psychiatric institution].[2]

Binck Bank may continue to use the word "turbo" to describe a particular
type of investment product, says The Hague District Court. BNP Paribas
had filed interim injunction proceedings against the online investment bank
on the grounds that 'turbo' was a trademark. The court ruled, however, that
"turbo" must be seen as a generic name because it has become so widely
used. The ABN AMRO bank developed the products and passed them on
to the Scottish bank RBS, which later sold them to BNP Paribas.[3]

After a four-month trial, only two of five defendants in Britain's most prof-
itable insider-trading case were found guilty. Two financial professionals
accused of making 7.4 million pounds ($10.7 million) with three others
on confidential information about six stocks have been found guilty by a
London court, with the other men acquitted.[4]

The appeal court in The Hague has ruled that the prospectus issued by
Bouw State [real estate investment fund] was not misleading. The court's
judgment was made public by Jonald Bouwhuis, founder of Bouwhuis
Vastgoed, the real estate group that owns the fund, in a trade journal.
A bondholder had instituted complaint proceedings because the risks associated with the investment product were not adequately reflected in the prospectus. According to Bouwhuis, the appeal court dismissed this argument.
"The Public Prosecution Service had already decided that it would not start
an investigation," he says. He further claims that all the sums invested were
invested as outlined in the prospectus.[5]

The State is to pay €10 million to Norma, a foundation that promotes
the interests of artists. The foundation sued the State for loss of income
from the private copying levy. The Supreme Court ruled in favour of
Norma in March 2014. Now the State and the foundation have agreed on a
€10 million settlement. The suspension of the private copying levy, designed to

---

[2] Dutch daily newspaper *De Telegraaf*, 9 September 2014.
[3] Dutch daily newspaper *NRC Handelsblad*, 10 September 2014.
[4] *Independent*, 10 May 2016.
[5] Dutch daily newspaper *Het Financieele Dagblad*, 9 September 2014.

compensate musicians and actors for loss of income through illegal down-loading, was what prompted Norma to start proceedings against the State.[6]

The task of the judiciary is not only to protect citizens from government, but to protect citizens, companies, other organisations and government authorities from each other. If you have a dispute with another individual, for instance, you can always apply to the courts, which will attempt to come to a just solution based on the rules of law. A home owner who is dissatisfied with renovation work done on her house can compel the contractor, through the courts, to improve the work done or to pay compensation. A policy holder who believes the insurance company should cover damage done to his car can go to court if necessary. If a customer fails to pay, the retailer can compel her to settle the bill. These are just some of the hundreds of thousands of cases that come before the courts. And the courts offer protection to both sides. They ensure that a person accused of a criminal offence gets a fair trial, but they also protect the victim. Such protection may take the form of a conviction, but the courts can also admit a claim from the victim in the same proceedings or order the defendant to pay compensation. The victim can of course apply directly to the civil courts for restitution.

The courts offer everyone the protection which the law provides for. 'Everyone' includes unpopular minorities, or people the public regard with loudly articulated dislike or even disgust. Judges apply the law equally to everyone even when the mob (or today, the internet) is baying for punishment without even considering the law.

Judges are confronted every day with people manifesting a wide range of qualities—goodness, evil, powerlessness, courage etc—and rarely on the happiest days of their lives. They see con artists, tax cheats, couples involved in marital conflict, businesses with large and small claims, murderers, people with learning difficulties, children, individuals embroiled in a dispute with their local authority, drug addicts and dealers, traffic offenders, and so on. A procession of individuals of all types and from all walks of life come to plead their case: municipal, provincial and central government officials, asylum seekers, representatives of multinationals, shopkeepers and other business people. In short, the whole of society appears before the judiciary, with or without representation.

[6] Dutch news website, www.nu.nl, accessed 9 September 2014.

II. THE JUDGE AS CRAFTSMAN: STRIKES
AND LEAF LETTUCE

Two examples:

> During the planned strike at the AkzoNobel industrial chemicals factory near Rotterdam production may not fall below 40% of capacity due to safety and environmental concerns. This was the decision yesterday of Rotterdam District Court in the interim injunction proceedings brought by AkzoNobel and two of its customers. The strike is scheduled to start at 6 a.m. on Monday morning and will last a week. AkzoNobel had asked the court to ban the strike or limit it to five days, but the court refused to comply. However, it granted one of the company's demands, ordering that chlorine production must not fall below 40% because this would lead to an increased risk of problems in the production process.[7]

> A market gardener was acquitted by the Hague Court of Appeal in a prosecution for economic offences. The charge was that in breach of the legislation, his lettuce contained excessive amounts of nitrate. But the lettuce in question was a type known as 'leaf lettuce'. The appeal court held that it was unclear whether leaf lettuce was covered by the legislation. The rules were therefore too vague and the defendant was acquitted. The Supreme Court took a different view. It decided that it was necessary to determine whether leaf lettuce could be considered a sub-category of ordinary lettuce. If that was the case, then it was enough for the legislator to criminalise the main category. Sometimes the legislator has to adopt a degree of vagueness in defining offences to prevent acts which should be penalised falling outside the scope of the definition. Vagueness may indeed be unavoidable, since it is not always possible to anticipate the way in which the interests to be protected could be damaged in the future and, where this can be anticipated, the definitions risk becoming so detailed that there is no overview, undermining the overall clarity of legislation. So who knows that too much nitrate in leaf lettuce is forbidden? Not the average consumer certainly, who need not fear arrest on leaving the supermarket with his lettuce. However, professional commercial parties, such as the market gardener in this case, may be expected to keep themselves informed of the restrictions imposed on their conduct.[8]

The law is the judiciary's toolkit. Most of the law judges have to apply is embodied in legislation, their primary yardstick. So the first

---

[7] Dutch daily newspaper *Reformatorisch Dagblad*, 9 September 2014; Rotterdam District Court, 5 September 2014.

[8] Dutch Supreme Court, 31 October 2000.

step is usually to study the legislation. On the face of it, that seems straightforward, but often isn't. An Act of Parliament may be complex in itself, and may furthermore refer to more detailed rules set out in secondary legislation. It may then be quite a job to establish which rule applies to a particular case, as in the story of the market gardener above.

The rules at issue there derived from an Act of Parliament, were worked out in detail in a decree relating specifically to the preparation and treatment of foodstuffs, and in even greater detail in a ministerial order on nitrate levels in vegetables. And that order was later amended by two other orders.

As we know, the courts have to take account of international treaties (like the European Convention on Human Rights) as well as national legislation. The Convention states, for example, that everyone has a right to a fair trial where their civil rights are at issue or if a criminal charge is brought against them. Statutory provisions are sometimes inconsistent or conflicting. Or a judge may be confronted with new situations that the law does not regulate. This happened when the fax and later email were introduced. The courts then have to fill the gaps in the legislation and reconcile clashing provisions. Sometimes the legislator has deliberately left the judiciary plenty of room to manoeuvre, as illustrated in the section in Chapter 5 on government criminal liability.

In some cases the law and the treaties are silent, so the judiciary has no yardstick provided by the legislator or the international community. In a number of these situations, the legislator has even explicitly stated that an issue must be assessed according to the principles of good faith and fair dealings. This was discussed earlier in Chapter 3 (judicial lawmaking and open norms). In such cases the court may look to see if previous judgments in comparable cases provide guidance. Or it may assess the matter in light of general principles of law, such as the proportionality principle (don't use a sledgehammer to crack a nut). This is what happened in the case of the strike at the chemicals factory described above. Although the right to strike is recognised in general terms in the European Social Charter, it is not worked out in detail either in the Charter or in Dutch legislation. Which is why in such cases the courts look at how other courts, including the Supreme Court, have ruled in the past.

In all these situations judges are required to display craftsmanship. They endeavour to get to the bottom of the facts presented in court.

Like a carpenter they measure, saw, fit and tighten the screws. Then they have to discover which rule of law applies to the case at hand, That also demands craftsmanship. They must know which written rules are relevant, whether there is previous case law, more specifically that of the highest court in the country and the two highest European courts: the European Court of Human Rights and the Court of Justice of the European Union. They must be familiar with general principles of law such as proportionality (the means must be proportionate to the end) and subsidiarity (principle of minimum coercion). The latter principle means that a strike, to take our example, should be a method of last resort and announced in a timely manner. The proportionality principle means that the court has to weigh the interests of one party (the strikers) against those of the other party (the company). The strikers have an interest in their wage demands being met, while in this case the company had an interest in preventing chlorine production being halted, which would additionally present risks to public health. On the basis of written and unwritten rules the court tries to reach a solution. The decision lies in its hands. Sometimes, if the law does not point clearly in one direction or another, it may choose to compromise. Which is what happened in the case of the strike described here: the workers were allowed to strike as long as production did not fall below 40%, because then it would become dangerous.

III. THE JUDICIARY HAS NO POLITICAL PROGRAMME:
KENNEDY AND OBAMA

> I believe in a president whose religious views are his own private affair [...] Whatever issue may come before me as president—on birth control, divorce, censorship, gambling or any other subject—I will make my decision [...] in accordance with what my conscience tells me to be the national interest, and without regard to outside religious pressures or dictates.[9]

These were the words of John Kennedy in 1960, while still a senator. President Barack Obama, on the other hand, once said that 'as progressives, we cannot abandon the field of religious discourse'. He went on: 'The discomfort of some progressives with any hint of religion has

---

[9] From a speech given by Senator John F. Kennedy to the Greater Houston Ministerial Association, 12 September 1960.

often prevented us from effectively addressing issues in moral terms'. Indeed, Obama believes that if liberals can only offer a political discourse 'scrubbed [...] of all religious content, we forfeit the imagery and terminology through which millions of Americans understand both their personal morality and social justice'.[10]

I doubt whether Kennedy's argument still holds for politicians. As we saw, President Obama's thinking on this subject is very different, allowing a prominent role for politicians' own beliefs and convictions. Although admittedly, in the 2004 US Senate election campaign, he made a comment more in line with Kennedy's views. In response to criticism that he was not behaving as a Christian, he replied 'that I was running to be the U.S. Senator of Illinois and not the Minister of Illinois'.[11]

These contrasting statements by Kennedy and Obama illustrate radically differing views on the relationship between politics and faith or moral convictions. They strengthen me in my view of where the judiciary must stand. Which is in the position chosen by Kennedy.

Unlike politicians, judges have no political programme that determines their preferences. They must constantly be on their guard against personal opinions, political or ideological bias, preconceived notions or views that seem self-evident. Judges must always be aware that they have not been appointed to propagate their personal preferences, to ride their own hobbyhorses, or to incorporate their own philosophies into their judgments. They are there to apply the law. And the law is not what they think it should be, perhaps on the basis of their consciences. Of course, the law may coincide with judges' personal convictions. But wherever the law allows them a degree of latitude, they must take care not to fall back too quickly on the choice those convictions would dictate, let alone to give them priority over the requirements of legislation, international agreements or general principles of law. Or, as former associate justice Louis Brandeis once said 'We must be ever on our guard, lest we erect our prejudices into legal principles'.[12] In this I differ from the renowned German author and constitutional judge Bernhard Schlink, who in 2010, during a debate held in the Peace Palace

[10] Keynote speech at Call to Renewal's *Building a Covenant for a New America* conference in Washington DC, 2006.

[11] As related by Obama himself in the same keynote speech.

[12] Quoted in S Breyer 2006, op. cit., p 19.

in the Hague, forecast that 'supreme and constitutional courts will become stronger and stronger, they will play an ever more active role and they will interfere more often and more resolutely in the political process'. I do not subscribe to this view nor would I applaud such a development.[13]

Judges try to understand and allow consideration of new, unexpected arguments presented to them. In brief, they both want and are compelled to adopt a fresh, unbiased attitude every day. Any judge who claimed to perform his duties on the basis of social democrat, liberal or religious convictions would be failing to understand and indeed undermining his position. That is why I am opposed to the idea of nominating judges on the basis of their political affiliations. As Supreme Court President I was in fact happy not to know the political preferences of candidates I presented to the House of Representatives. The politician wants to achieve something, wants to help society to progress. In a certain sense—but only in a certain sense—the judge wants nothing. He listens, reads, lets the arguments sink in, wonders if there are not perhaps other arguments that are relevant. And then he reaches a decision, with all due respect for the arguments advanced. Judges are thus, as it were, unprogrammed.[14] Yet before giving judgment, they have been dealing with politically sensitive matters such as public safety, the multicultural society and the financial system. And they have to decide, they cannot refuse.

If judges have no political programme, does that mean they have no objectives? Indeed they do. Their task is to strive for justice in the specific cases that come before them. This they have undertaken to do. But this task is not a programme offering exact guidance on how to adjudicate in practice. The main yardstick, as I said earlier, is the law as it is embodied in legislation, international agreements, case law and unwritten rules of law. The task commits judges first and foremost to procedural correctness. That is not just a formal duty: it compels judges to weigh all the interests involved. Once again and in the simplest of terms, the work of the judge is to administer justice in specific cases. Of course, the reference framework and judges' social context play a

---

[13] Bernhard Schlink and Geert Corstens, 'Objective law and subjective judges', Cossee, Amsterdam 2011, p 76.

[14] H Gommer, *Onder de rechter* (Sub judice—in Dutch), thesis, Tilburg, Nijmegen, Wolf, 2008, p 33, speaks of 'disinterest'.

role, consciously or not. But they must always guard against that role becoming predominant. As I have said before, they are not appointed to impose their personal opinions.[15] Like other public servants—the name says it all—judges serve the community. Their endeavour must be to ensure that the peaceful life of society, of citizens, companies and institutions, runs as smoothly as possible, each respecting the other's position. In this complex framework the role they must play is that of the just judge.

IV. JUDGES LISTEN AND DECIDE: LET BOTH SIDES BE HEARD

As someone once wrote to me, 'Listening means putting yourself in the other person's place, without getting in the way yourself. It means being open and accommodating, and respecting the other person. Another person's opinion is often much more interesting than your own: you're familiar with that already'. There is much in this that applies to judges. Of course, in a purely commercial dispute, for example about failure to deliver a consignment of vegetables, it may be less relevant. But even there, the judge must make the effort to understand the conflict and clearly establish the facts. And in cases of a more personal nature, these words hold particularly true. The judge must hear *and* listen, must read *and* understand: these are not synonyms. Like a good doctor listening to a patient, the judge must be able to put himself in the other's shoes, hear her standpoint and try to get to the heart of the matter.

In many cases the parties appear in person to be heard by the court. In some cases the proceedings are purely written. In yet other cases only counsel for either side speak. But in all cases the judge has to allow the arguments presented by the parties to sink in. And experience shows that judges must never form a judgment after hearing only one of the parties. They know that if you have heard one side of the argument, the standpoint may seem reasonable, but hearing the other side can create a very different picture. Even in matters of life and death. For example, the public prosecutor accuses someone of murder and explains the facts. But once the court has heard the defendant, even if they confess

---

[15] Parts of the preceding passages are taken from my inaugural address as president of the Supreme Court, *Prudence et audace* (Prudence and courage), *Nederlands Juristenblad* 2008, pp 2526–2529.

to the crime, there may turn out to be mitigating circumstances. This happens in other areas of law too, of course, such as granting custody of children to the father or mother or if one party has failed to fulfil the terms of a contract. As the Latin says, *audi et alteram partem*—let the other side be heard. This is an ancient principle of fundamental justice, of crucial importance to every judge.

V. THE JUDICIARY AND THE MEDIA:
TWITTER AND TWEETING

> The world around us, seen through our own eyes or the multifocal lenses of the media, is an amazing place. The law and legal practice can benefit in all kinds of ways from the opportunities presented by modern media. Detection, communication, freedom of information, knowledge acquisition, new forms of dispute settlement and mediation, professional and personal interaction, all these things become easier and more accessible as long as you can find your way in the new technological landscape. What is more, the increasing number of "senders" in modern media makes it possible for justice authorities and legal entities to have much more control over the way in which they come across to their "receivers". And it is crucial that legal professionals realise that what matters is not how useful the media are to them but what message they have for the public.[16]

Basically, you can allow yourself to get frustrated by what you read in social media, or you can take advantage of it. The Dutch Supreme Court did this as early as 2010, when I started to tweet. I decided to send alerts to our followers when important judgments were published, having already organised the publication of press releases ahead of upcoming rulings. And nowadays, as soon as a judgment is pronounced in open court, it appears on the internet accompanied by a more simply worded summary or press release. At this point a judge responsible for public relations is available to answer questions about the ruling. Sometimes—in extremely important cases like the fire at Schiphol airport in October 2005 where 11 irregular migrants detained there lost their lives—the Court puts a video interview with this same judge on the internet. In a sense, the Supreme Court has taken control of its media presence. Since 2005, other courts have followed suit. And at the

---

[16] Gerben Kor, *De togakamer* (The robing room—in Dutch), p 15.

same time, the Supreme Court maintains an honest and open relationship with the media. It is clear that there is enormous public interest in court judgments. This is a positive sign. Just as people like to know what the first and second branches of government (the legislature and the executive) are doing, they are equally interested in the daily work of the third branch, the judiciary. It is also important for judges not to regard journalists as enemies, but instead to help them in news gathering and in formulating their message. Journalism plays a vital role in a democratic society. Since we changed our public relations system and began providing journalists with easy-to-read abstracts, opening today's newspaper and wondering whether what you decided the day before is accurately reflected is a thing of the past.

Finally, it is important for judges to underpin their rulings with clearly reasoned arguments. Though changes have been made, rulings still contain sentences that are long and difficult to unravel. That can and should be improved. And perhaps we should explain the background in the decision itself a little more than we do at present. Fortunately, as I said just now, in the Netherlands the most important decisions are nowadays accompanied by a summary formulated in a simpler style. It is essential for the public to understand what is happening in the administration of justice.

VI. ONCE AGAIN: JUDGES MUST BE BRAVE

Just another news item, this time from a local newspaper:

> Oud-Alblas—On Wednesday 26 February (2014) the single judge trying criminal cases acquitted a 23-year-old man from Oud-Alblas accused of burglary and the theft of audio equipment from a storage facility. The court found the evidence unconvincing. Three co-defendants were convicted last year; two received community service orders of 80 hours, one of 40 hours. [...] The judge went on to say 'When I compare your statements as defendant against those of your three co-defendants, the doubt this causes me means that the cards fall your way. I am not entirely persuaded that what the prosecutor has charged you with is in fact what happened. I am therefore acquitting you'.

The following reactions were posted on the newspaper's website:

> Beer Glass: Yeah, yeah, how naive can you get?? No wonder nobody trusts the courts.

Rumblestiltskin: They're all criminals there anyway.

Derek: Ridiculously low sentence. Crime rewarded yet again.

The Sandman: And then they get a cup of coffee and a hug. And of course compensation. Does ANYBODY still believe in the legal system?

Tu: Why don't people read the whole item? It says this guy denied everything, right from the beginning. So he won't have given any names. The other defendants did name him, probably so they could share the costs. So in my opinion these three are trying to screw him. And what low sentence? Acquittal is not a sentence, the judge acquitted him, so he's innocent. And whether I believe in the legal system—yes I do, these people went to college to become judges and prosecutors, which is more than I can apparently say for most visitors to this site!

Poopie: Get a grip Rumblestiltskin. What d'you mean by 'there'?

It is no rare occurrence for the public to react in this way to rulings. Sometimes people find it hard to understand why a person has been acquitted, illustrated here by the dissatisfaction expressed by Beer Glass, Derek and The Sandman. Tu points to the role of the judge, who clearly explained why he was going to acquit the defendant: because he was not convinced that he committed the offence. He applied a legal rule which says that it must be both lawfully and convincingly established that the defendant committed the crime with which he is charged. Only if these conditions have been fulfilled can the court convict and sentence. So the legislator has told the judge that if there is doubt, he must acquit. For where there is doubt, the court cannot be convinced.

Besides dissatisfaction with poorly understood acquittals, the public often expresses concern about sentencing: penalties are perceived as too low and the courts as too mild. In the example above, Derek represents this line of thinking. He was probably referring to the sentences the co-defendants received. In imposing sentences, the court takes account of the circumstances in which the offence was committed and the character and personal circumstances of the defendant.

If a first offender holds up a service station, for example, he may receive a fairly long custodial sentence which is partially suspended. The part that is not suspended is equal to the time spent on remand. Say that that was six months. The defendant is released on the day judgment is pronounced. One of the factors involved in such a decision is that the court may have wished to prevent a first offender spending a long time in prison—that can lead to more serious offending. In addition, society benefits if the penalty imposed helps put the offender back on the right track. In addition to a partially suspended sentence, the court can impose a community service order for a substantial number of hours. So the offender is given a chance, but knows that if he commits another offence within a specified period (the 'operational period'), the suspended part of the first custodial sentence will be added to any penalty imposed for the second offence. Additional conditions may be attached to a suspended sentence, like compulsory meetings with a probation officer, or a course of treatment or training. Penalties can thus be tailored to fit both offence and offender. This is what sometimes causes public concern. Partly because in the media, a whole package as described here is summed up as 'armed robbers get community service order—again'. At receptions and parties judges are often tackled on this question. Many try to remain aloof, saying that without personal knowledge of the case or the defendant they cannot express an opinion. And knowledge is exactly what the judges hearing the case have. They have studied the case file, in many cases have come face-to-face with defendants and sometimes have further information about their personal circumstances through a psychiatric or probation service report.

A study carried out by psychology professor Willem Wagenaar, supervised by a committee I chaired, came up with some very interesting results. It involved lay persons in current criminal proceedings. On the morning preceding the hearing they were allowed to look at the most important documents in the case file and attended the hearing itself in the afternoon. They then proceeded to discuss the case at the same time as the judges, but in a different room. Finally, their views on the sentences to be imposed were compared. The sentences proposed by the participants were not significantly heavier than those imposed by the judges, though the professionals were slightly more likely to acquit, being a little more cautious than the lay 'judges'. You could conclude therefore that the difference of opinion concerning the severity of sentences disappears if ordinary people have access to the same information as judges.[17] There was no 'sentencing gap'. Of course, this

---

[17] W A Wagenaar, *Strafrechtelijke oordelen van rechters en leken* (Differences between judges and lay persons in terms of sentencing—in Dutch), Council for the Judiciary, Research Memoranda no 2, year 4, 2008.

does not mean there is no gap in real life. Not everyone can have the experience that the study participants had. The impression that judges impose excessively mild sentences will thus persist as long as they take the circumstances of the case and the defendant into account. Which is what they must continue to do.

So any rules of law limiting judges' ability to tailor the sentence to the character of the defendant and the offence in question that might be introduced have a number of disadvantages. It would be unfortunate if the introduction of such measures, including minimum sentences or a ban on community service orders, was based on an erroneous impression of sentencing and thus offered a solution for a non-existent problem.

VII. JUDGES MUST RETAIN A CERTAIN DISTANCE: COURT FEES AND ATTITUDE

Judges must ensure that their independence and impartiality cannot be doubted. The way to do this, as professionals, is to keep political considerations at arm's length. Whether they can take up a seat in the upper house of parliament or on a local authority council depends on how this is regulated in each country. In the Netherlands it is not formally prohibited, but even if judges who are thus members of a legislative assembly explicitly refrain from getting involved in matters relating to the administration of justice, it can still be said that the party they represent voted for a particular item of legislation. They have constantly to be aware that a political conflict can metamorphose into a legal dispute which may be presented to them in court. If a judge takes on the role of politician, he may get in his colleagues' way. Even worse, opponents of measures agreed by the legislature will see him as no longer impartial if he has to decide in a dispute concerning those measures. It is better to avoid such situations. Whenever I have been consulted on draft legislation, I have nearly always confined myself to technical considerations. I only felt free to take up a more decided position if a bill seriously undermined achievements of the rule of law. One example was the Dutch government's plan to substantially increase court fees. Together with the Procurator General, I opposed this plan. Contrary to what is customary, we published our advisory opinion. On the other hand, when the government proposed to make retrial possible following acquittal, we confined ourselves to technical issues. It was a highly sensitive issue, politically, but it did not impact on the achievements of the rule of law. Many countries, including in Western Europe, have such a system of retrial after acquittal.

In other ways, too, judges must keep a distance. They understand society better than most (see Chapter 6) because they operate in its midst. This does not mean that they constantly have to demonstrate this. An open attitude is good, but getting too close to socially or politically sensitive issues can undermine their independence and impartiality. They must ensure that literally everyone can rely on them, regardless of social position (however different from theirs), political creed (however far from theirs), and religious or ideological conviction (however far removed from theirs). Such factors must not stand in the way of the judiciary performing its role independently and without bias.

VIII. IMAGE AND REALITY: WEST WING AND 'SOFT' JUDGES

'I don't care what it is, I care what it looks like!' says the White House press secretary in one of the earliest episodes of the TV series *West Wing*. Public image is a significant factor in creating public support and would seem to be influencing the choices made by policymakers to an ever-increasing extent. Why should this worry us? For example, misconceptions regarding the severity of sentences could lead to legislation limiting the judiciary's ability to tailor the penalty to the perpetrator and the offence. I don't expect Germany, France, the Netherlands and other European countries to introduce a 'three strikes and you're out' system like the one they have in California, which makes life imprisonment mandatory after a third conviction for a violent or serious felony. But even less radical restrictions on tailoring sentences like (in England and Wales) introducing a range of mandatory minimum sentences, including the possibility, in certain cases, of mandatory sentences of life imprisonment can have unfavourable effects in individual cases. If the erroneous impression that sentencing cannot be left to overly 'soft' judges is not corrected, legislation could be passed which will hinder rather than help judges to perform their task properly.

What is more, the judiciary is obliged to base that performance on reality, not on the notion the public has, or has been fed, of the facts of the case and those involved. The words of the *West Wing* press secretary are practically a cliché these days: image is becoming more important to people than reality. How often do we hear 'Focus on how you come across, not on who you are'? This may well be important to get your audience on your side. But it is not how a judge (or a politician or a member of the executive) should behave. In this context, the judge has it easier than the politicians, who sooner or later start thinking about the next election and perhaps shaping their behaviour accordingly. Judges don't face this problem, being appointed for life, at least in many countries. They have no voters to please, though they do have to ensure that the public continues to accept them. Any court system that moves further and further away from the people will eventually lose legitimacy in their eyes. This must be avoided, but not by bowing to the prevailing—or the most stridently announced—social trend. My advice to the judiciary would be to develop a good press policy. Explain clearly what you do and why you do it. Give justice a human face. Publish readable summaries of your judgments. Avoid arrogance. Raise a dissenting voice where necessary and do it in a way that people understand. For example, try to counter the stubborn misconception that criminal judges are too soft.[18] The work of the judiciary must be explained. Judgments and camera coverage of proceedings cannot just be sent out into the world. That's of no use to anyone. Knowledge of the context is vital if people are to understand: it's pointless to show someone a CO_2 catalytic converter without mentioning that it is part of a vehicle's exhaust system. It is the judiciary's responsibility to ensure that the general public and journalists have access to sound, comprehensible information about the administration of justice. In the US, the Michael Jackson Trial App topped the Apple charts. Should we in Europe aspire to this?

Over the years, the Dutch courts have steadily improved the readability of the reasoning underpinning their judgments. Anyone who checks out their website will probably be pleasantly surprised by the comprehensibility of the rulings posted there. Courts use Twitter and publish press releases, designated judges and public prosecutors talk to the media and information is made available to the public in all sorts of ways, from open days to reconstructions of cases using Playmobil.

---

[18] In the Netherlands at least, this is certainly a misconception. For a comparison of the Dutch courts with criminal courts in other European countries see WODC, 'Criminaliteit en rechtshandhaving 2012' (Crime and law enforcement 2012—in Dutch), Ch 11, *Nederland in internationaal perspectief* (The Netherlands from an international perspective—in Dutch), The Hague, BJU 2012.

IX. CRITICISM OF THE JUDICIARY: THE VIRTUE OF MODERATION

Linked with the above is another issue close to my heart. Representatives of the three branches of government should not make statements that undermine public confidence in the institutions of a state governed by the rule of law. And they have a responsibility to exercise restraint in their responses, particularly to incidents. During the proceedings against the Dutch political leader Geert Wilders, I spoke out on television. This was prompted by his statement that should he be convicted of discrimination against Muslims, millions of people would no longer trust the judiciary. I felt obliged to speak up because a member of parliament must obey the Constitution and the values it enshrines. One of those values is the balance of powers and respect for the institutions of the state. Recently I spoke out again when this same leader, once again facing prosecution for discrimination against Muslims, expressed doubts both in and outside the court regarding the integrity of the judges. A defendant is to a certain extent free to criticise the bench. But a defendant who is also a member of parliament should not sow the seeds of doubt among his followers concerning the integrity of judges. A second reason why politicians should not make statements that undermine public confidence in the judiciary is that it is hard for judges to react in public to those statements. They always have to be aware that the same issue may come up in proceedings. The parties might doubt a judge's impartiality if he or she has already commented on that issue in public. A certain distance must always be maintained. I realised that by commenting on television on the words of this political leader I would no longer be in a position to judge his case in the Supreme Court. I would be considered insufficiently impartial. Fortunately, the first case did not come before the Supreme Court. And by the time the second case was being heard, I was no longer chief justice. So, my colleagues still sitting on the bench might have been pleased that somebody who no longer runs the risk of being accused of lack of impartiality took a stand.

Furthermore, the legislature and the executive should not saddle the judiciary with measures appearing to promote safety and security which are unenforceable, so that the courts get the blame. For example, if more funding for the police predictably leads to an increase in the number of cases, the capacity of the prosecution authorities and the courts will have to increase too.

This does not mean that judges cannot be criticised. The judiciary is open to criticism: in fact, the whole system of appeal is based on judges' awareness of their own fallibility. Criticism keeps us on our toes, but in public debate it should be expressed with due respect for the position of members of the judiciary. Untimely or unthinking criticism damages the institution and can distort the balance between the three branches of government. Maybe you remember the former Italian prime minister who made a habit of fulminating against the judiciary. He called prosecutors and judges 'the cancer of democracy'. My answer to that is, yes, just as the right to vote is a cancer, and Big Bird is a menace to our economy, as Obama joked in a re-election campaign advert.[19] But such statements about the justice authorities are not peculiar to Italy. Politicians in the Netherlands have also advocated sacking judges who hand down judgments they do not like. A presidential candidate who lost a procedure in a federal court criticised the judge by stating: 'I have a judge who is a hater of Donald Trump. A hater. He's a hater,' Trump said. 'We're in front of a very hostile judge. The judge was appointed by Barack Obama,' Such a statement is far from being appropriate and undermines the judiciary.[20] Of course the government must respond when people have justified concerns about public safety. And of course there must be room for the victim in criminal proceedings. And of course my first reaction when I read of jewellers being raided time and time again is anger. I too sometimes think: lock them up and throw away the key. But it is precisely the job of the judiciary not to convert these very human and comprehensible responses into a judgment, but to be aware of the all circumstances of the case. Judges who do their job properly and arrive at balanced decisions—which as the statistics show, may often involve imposing a heavy sentence—deserve respect and support.

What I am trying to say here is that if judges worry about politicians or other opinion makers who utter sweeping condemnations of their rulings, it is not because they are too thin-skinned.

---

[19] www.youtube.com/watch?v=bZxs09eV-Vc.
[20] *Huffington Post*, 29 May 2016.

7

Guaranteeing the Quality of Justice

Lucia de Berk acquitted

Arnhem—Last Wednesday an unusual scene unfolded in the court building in Arnhem: the packed public gallery applauded as one when the appeal court removed the label of "serial murderess" from Lucia de Berk. According to the court, it cannot be proven that the "victims" died as a result of human intervention, let alone that De Berk had anything to do with their deaths. The 48-year-old was acquitted on seven counts of murder and three of attempted murder of hospital patients. She had been sentenced to life imprisonment for these offences on the basis, as it later transpired, of unsound evidence. De Berk has always claimed she is innocent. The acquittal on Wednesday means that she is fully rehabilitated.

The miscarriage of justice that took place in the Lucia de Berk case is not the first [in the Netherlands]. The Schiedam park murder and the Putten murder are other cases where the wrong people ended up behind bars.[1]

Child abuse trial judge accused of being drunk in court. Crown court judge Douglas Field freed alleged paedophile while apparently "influenced by alcohol", according to victim's mother.

The legal watchdog is investigating a crown court judge after he was accused of being "influenced by alcohol" during a trial in which an alleged paedophile was freed. Judge Douglas Field, 63, is said to have attended a leaving party during an extended lunch break. He then instructed his jury to acquit a 55-year-old defendant accused of raping an eight-year-old, after they failed to reach a verdict at the end of the five-day hearing. It is claimed, however, that Field forgot the man was facing a further two charges and dismissed the jury before they were able to give their verdict.[2]

Angry judge assaults train conductor.

"The judge is extremely upset about what happened. So upset that she cannot speak to the media at the moment." Reurt Gisolf, president of the

[1] Dutch daily newspaper *De Telegraaf*, 14 April 2010.
[2] *The Guardian*, 8 April 2011.

Amsterdam district court, is refusing to allow the press to contact the judge and vice-president of the court, who this week struck a train conductor in the face. "All I can say is that she is very sorry for what she has done. It should never have happened," he continued.

Last Tuesday the NS rail company carried out ticket checks at Amsterdam-Zuid station, close to the court building. Seven conductors stood at the bottom of the escalator leading to the platforms and asked to see passengers' tickets. The new travel rules mean that checks sometimes take place before passengers get on the train. The judge had to find her ticket in her bag. She reacted with irritation because the train was already standing at the platform. The conductor remarked that she should have left work earlier. The judge did in fact miss her train and was so angry that she ran back to the conductor and relieved her feelings by striking him in the face. The man suffered bruising to his cheek and jaw. As an NS spokesperson put it, "She gave him a hell of a blow".

What the judge did not know was that the conductor in question had undergone surgery recently for a herniated disc in his neck. The blow touched on sensitive nerves. He immediately called in sick and according to the NS is extremely distressed by the judge's aggressiveness. It was only when she was taken by the railway police for interview at the police station that it emerged that she was a vice-president of the district court.

The police report was sent to the Supreme Court, which will ask a public prosecutor working outside Amsterdam to handle the case. The judge may not have to appear in court. 'Common assault' is often settled by means of a payment in lieu of prosecution.

The NS however is contemplating suing the judge for compensation, both on account of the conductor's injuries, and the company's own losses because he has to take time off.[3]

I. LUCIA DE BERK, THE DRUNKEN JUDGE AND THE PUGNACIOUS JUDGE

THE PREVIOUS CHAPTERS have made it clear that being a judge is no soft option. The work carries many responsibilities and is highly demanding. To meet those demands, the first requirement of course is that capable people are selected and trained.

---

[3] Dutch daily newspaper *Trouw*, 9 June 1995.

They must then be enabled to do their work properly and keep their knowledge up to date. But even then, judges are not machines. So the administration of justice will never be perfect. It can in fact go very wrong, especially when substantial interests are involved. The only thing we can do is build in certain safety features. When mistakes are made—someone is wrongly convicted, or wrongly acquitted, a judge makes a serious error of law, or overlooks important arguments put by one of the parties—the system must offer ways of correcting the mistake. This is why we have a range of legal remedies: a judgment can be appealed, and thereafter taken to the highest court in the country. One might call these ordinary legal remedies. In addition, there are extraordinary remedies, the most well-known (applied in cases like that of Lucia de Berk) being retrial.

Alongside the remedies you can employ to challenge the decision in your case, it is also possible to complain about the judges. Being only human, they can make mistakes or become dysfunctional. A variety of sanctions are possible, in the worst case scenario even dismissal.

I would now like to look at the 'safety features' in the system that safeguard the quality of the administration of justice.

II. SELECTION, TRAINING AND FACILITATING GOOD WORK

In many countries you must have a law degree and undergo a stringent selection procedure to become a judge. In the Netherlands there is a national selection committee whose members are drawn from various walks of life: public administration, business, education and research, the Bar and the judiciary. Psychological and IQ tests form part of the selection procedure. Those who make it through the procedure then receive on-the-job training. Depending on the work experience the trainee judge already has, this stage can last from 18 months to four years. In this period the trainee judge acquires a huge amount of knowledge and a variety of skills: how to handle proceedings, how to write a good judgment, how to deal with difficult defendants or witnesses etc. In some countries an examination has to be passed before trainees are admitted to the judiciary.

As in many other professions it is important, once embarked on a career as a judge, to keep abreast of new developments. The law is in a state of constant evolution. New legislation is introduced, old laws lapse. Every week, the European courts and the highest national court publish rulings that are often relevant to many similar cases; at the same time, social and scientific developments are sometimes crucial to the law.

For straightforward cases that involve, say, the theft of a bicycle or a conifer planted too close to the boundary of a property, this has no serious implications. At least, from the technical point of view. But the human aspects of such cases often demand tact and empathy.

There are also highly specialised areas of law. Think for example of cases involving breaches of trademark rights, company law, customs and excise law, insurance issues in intercontinental shipping, etc. In each case, judges are often faced with parties who deal with the matter at issue on a daily basis. This is a challenging situation: judges will need to deploy a great deal of expertise if they are to arrive at a sound ruling. Proper information from the parties is therefore even more important than usual.

To ensure that the judiciary does not fall behind in the face of the specialisation seeping into every corner of society, most countries have introduced specialised courts. These cover the main areas of law: civil, criminal, tax and administrative law. Within these larger areas there are further specialisms. And in many countries courts have been scaled up in recent years and employ larger numbers of judges. This makes further specialisation easier. In the past, a court might hear only a handful of cases in a specific field, so that spending a lot of resources on keeping judicial officers up-to-date on that specialised knowledge was inefficient. The aim of scaling-up was to promote quality and efficiency.

A high-quality legal system is of vital importance to society. Judges must be enabled to provide that quality. They try to work speedily, but quality demands time. A couple of years ago, the workload of the Dutch courts, particularly the criminal courts, became the subject of public debate, set in motion by a number of justices from the Leeuwarden appeal court after the problems had been aired several times in the professional literature. It is now absolutely clear that the alarm sounded in the justices' manifesto (and supported by many judges) regarding the imminent loss of quality because of production pressures was well founded. As justice Fred Hammerstein commented, 'You don't ask a cardiac surgeon to do the operation in half the time'.

Following the publication of the manifesto, I wrote an article in two Dutch daily newspapers urging that the concerns it expressed should be taken seriously and properly investigated. The outcome could serve as a basis for a public and political debate on what we expect from our judiciary. Since then, much has happened. The Dutch Council for the Judiciary (the body which is partly responsible for managing the district and appeal courts) visited the courts and learned that the main concerns were unacceptably long working hours, lack of time for reflection and training, for consultation between colleagues and for permanent education, the extensive use of deputy judges for production reasons and discouragement of the deferral of cases.

Looking at this list of problems, it doesn't take long to realise that if they persist within the judicial organisation for any length of time, the results could be disastrous. Of course timely disposal of cases is an important element of quality. If judges and prosecutors have to work long hours from time to time, that is part of the job. And there may occasionally be no time in the working week for permanent education. But this should not become structural. Yet this was the situation in the Netherlands, according to a survey presented by the Dutch Association for the Judiciary in 2014.

A letter sent by the Council for the Judiciary on 21 February 2013 to all judges working in the courts under its management concluded that the overemphasis on production should be tackled. It also argued, correctly, that it was crucial for judges themselves to reach a consensus on what the proper administration of justice is in practice. They are responsible for developing and maintaining explicit, professional quality standards. Much hard work has gone into this since then. One aspect concerns establishing production norms on the basis of outcomes in recent time-on-task research.

In a word, many good things are happening, in close consultation with the judiciary. But we must remain alert and offer as much support as possible to our loyal, hard-working judges.

III. OPEN COURTS: KAFKA AND 'JANET AND JOHN SPEAK'

Transparency in the administration of justice has long been regarded as a guarantee of quality. It would seem only logical: if outsiders, or even those involved, cannot observe and monitor the work of the judiciary, if 'secret' decisions are made, we're on a slippery slope. Just read *The Trial* by Franz Kafka, one of the best-known novels in

European literature, which tells the tale of a man arrested and prosecuted by an inaccessible authority for a crime whose nature is never revealed. Or read Charles Dickens' *Bleak House* for an insight into a corrupt, dysfunctional court system shrouded in secrecy and inaccessible to ordinary people.

Open judicial proceedings have extra significance because judges, unlike politicians, cannot be called to account in the democratic process. In many cases a court ruling can be challenged in a higher court, but there is no other power in democratic states governed by the rule of law that can call the judiciary itself to account. It is openness that compensates for this lack of democratic scrutiny. It gives the people the opportunity to form an opinion on what the judiciary does and to express criticism. Judges will probably take such criticism to heart, but they are not obliged to.

More important perhaps is the pre-emptive effect of openness. The judge presiding over the hearing must take the presence of the public into account, an extra incentive for proper conduct. And his judgment will be published, so he has to allow for the fact that criticism may ensue. That may help him work in a disciplined manner. In short, an open legal system has many blessings.

IV. IS IT NECESSARY TO HAVE MORE TRANSPARENCY?

In the Netherlands, as in many other countries, the judiciary is one of the most transparent branches of government. Court sessions are open to the public. Judgments are pronounced in open court, underpinned with clear reasons and published. An effective media policy is in place (designated judges, prosecutors and justices deal with the media). A revolution has taken place in recent years—and now the Dutch Supreme Court even tweets.

I believe there is little room for improvement. Rulings must be comprehensible, but there is no need for 'Janet and John'-style language. If I had to point to an area where things could still improve, I would say that in some cases judgments could be better substantiated and that judges must be even more aware of the possible sensitivity of the issue they are adjudicating on. This doesn't mean that they have to alter their rulings because of public concern: where the decision itself is concerned, they have to remain independent, impartial and at arm's length.

But in the reasons they supply to underpin their rulings, they must take care not to overlook such sensitivities.

V. ORDINARY LEGAL REMEDIES: THE FIRE AT SCHIPHOL AIRPORT

Schiphol fire defendant acquitted on appeal.

The principal defendant in the case of the fire in the cell complex at Schiphol airport has been acquitted on all charges in appeal proceedings. According to the appeal court, Ahmed al-Jeballi, a failed Libyan asylum seeker, cannot be held responsible for the fire. Al-Jeballi, who was awaiting deportation, was initially sentenced to three years' imprisonment for deliberately causing the fire that broke out in the cells at Schiphol-Oost in 2005.

It has emerged from new investigations that intent to cause the fire could not be proven. On that basis, the Supreme Court ruled that the appeal proceedings had to be held afresh.[4]

In Chapter 2, I explained that most cases are initially heard by a court of first instance. If either party disagrees with that court's ruling, it can apply to the appeal court. This is the basic structure which can vary depending on the situation. The appeal court's judgment can be challenged before the highest court in a country. Applying to the appeal court and the highest court both come under what we call ordinary remedies, but they differ considerably from each other. In principle, a case can be heard entirely afresh in appeal proceedings, with a new assessment and possibly a new investigation of the facts. In Belgium, France, the Netherlands and some other Western European countries, appeals to the highest court only deal with questions of law. In brief, the court of first instance and the appeal courts hear the facts of the case, while the supreme courts deal with points of law. In these jurisdictions the latter are known as courts of cassation (from the Old French 'casser', meaning to annul, since this court can overturn the decisions of the courts hearing the facts). The court of cassation bases its assessment on the facts as established by the lower courts and only looks to see if the law (including procedural law) was correctly interpreted and

---

[4] Dutch weekly *Elsevier*, 1 March 2013.

applied, and if the judgment in question was sufficiently and comprehensibly substantiated. This means that the opportunities for having an earlier court ruling overturned in cassation are limited. The aim of cassation proceedings is to promote the uniformity of the law, to ensure its further development and to provide legal protection where necessary.

In the case of the Schiphol fire, each level of this structure came into play. The district court (court of first instance) convicted the defendant and sentenced him to three years in prison. He lodged an appeal, resulting in a reduced sentence of 18 months. The Supreme Court (court of cassation) overturned the appeal court ruling on the grounds that the court had given insufficient reasons for its refusal to allow the defence to appoint its own expert to carry out further investigations. These consisted of a statistical analysis of the chances that a cigarette butt thrown to the ground in the circumstances at issue could have been the cause of the fire. The Supreme Court ruled that such an analysis could have shed light on the question of whether the fire had been started deliberately. It thus contributed to the development of the law and offered legal protection. The appeal court that heard the case afresh acquitted Mr Al-Jeballi.[5]

VI. RETRIAL

In many countries it is possible to assess afresh a case in which a judgment convicting—and sometimes even acquitting—the defendant has become final, and therefore unappealable. This is known as a retrial.

In England, Wales and Northern Ireland, in the Netherlands and in many other countries, retrial is possible if new facts arise in a criminal case in which a conviction or acquittal has become final. These are thus facts of which the court was unaware and that give firm grounds for assuming that had they been known at the time, the court would have come to a different decision. Retrial is an exception to the general rule *lites finiri oportet* (the legal battle must end at some point).

In England and Wales, the Criminal Cases Review Commission decides on applications for retrial; in the Netherlands it is the highest court. If the Criminal Cases Review Commission or the Supreme Court

---

[5] The Hague Appeal Court, 1 March 2013.

grants such an application, the case is investigated and tried afresh. If the person concerned was convicted, this may lead to an acquittal, but also to the conviction being maintained if the original charge is found proven. A recent example in the UK was the case of Alexander Blackman, convicted of murder after shooting dead a wounded enemy combatant in Afghanistan on 15 September 2011. Following an in-depth investigation that lasted eleven months, the Criminal Cases Review Commission decided to refer the case to the Courts Martial Appeal Court. The referral was made on the basis of a number of grounds. These included the new evidence that emerged, including new expert evidence acquired by the Commission, relating to Mr Blackman's mental state at the time of the offence, and the fact that an alternative verdict of unlawful manslaughter was not available during the trial. The Commission concluded that these issues raised a real possibility that the Courts Martial Appeal Court would quash Mr Blackman's murder conviction.

If retrial is applied for in the case of an acquittal—a possibility in several countries like England and Wales, Germany and the Netherlands—this can ultimately lead to a conviction or to the acquittal being upheld.

VII. RECUSAL: BIASED JUDGES

Anyone involved in court proceedings who has good reasons for thinking that the judge cannot be impartial in his handling of the case may ask to have the judged replaced (or 'recused'). If for example it transpires that the judge is a former attorney and an ex-colleague from the same chambers is representing one of the parties, this may give cause to doubt his impartiality. Or if the judge is an ex-public prosecutor and the case is being heard in the same district, defence counsel may challenge him for bias. Such requests are granted in exceptional cases. If there really is a problem, the judge concerned will probably let his colleagues know at an early stage that he cannot hear the case. There is a special procedure for this. This possibility also exists in the UK.[6]

---

[6] The leading case is *Regina v Bow Street Metropolitan Stipendiary Magistrate and Others, ex pte Pinochet Ugarte* [2000] 1 A.C. 119.

VIII. HOW DO WE GET RID OF BAD JUDGES?

Judges are usually appointed for life, though the age of retirement differs from country to country. In many countries, including the Netherlands, they retire at seventy. Where such rules apply, judges cannot be suspended or dismissed by the government or parliament. Nevertheless, situations arise in which it must be possible to suspend or dismiss a judge, for example if they are physically or mentally unable to do their work or have been convicted of a serious offence. There are ways of doing this. In England, High Court Judges (meaning, broadly speaking, those who sit in any of the top three layers: Supreme Court, Court of Appeal or High Court) can only be removed by the Queen, after an address from both Houses of Parliament; other judges can be removed by the Lord Chancellor, with the concurrence of the Lord Chief Justice, for incapacity or misbehaviour. In the Netherlands the Procurator General at the Supreme Court can apply to have a judge suspended or dismissed. The Supreme Court decides. Such an application cannot be made on the grounds that a judge has made the wrong decision. The system of legal remedies is there to rectify this situation, to quash factually or legally incorrect rulings. The independence of the judiciary would be under threat if judges ran the risk of being sacked because they hand down a judgment which in their view is in accordance with the law, but is seen as incorrect by politicians and the public.

The Dutch Constitution stipulates that judges appointed for life may only be dismissed on grounds specified in legislation. There are two main categories. First, if they have acted in a way irreconcilable with judicial office: for example if they have committed a crime. Second, if they are unfit, on health or other grounds, to carry out their work. In practice this is a rare occurrence. A judge who knows he is about to be prosecuted for a serious offence will resign rather than wait to be dismissed. The Prosecutor General then has no reason for taking action.

The 2013 annual report of the Supreme Court listed the following cases.

> The Procurator General at the Supreme Court applied for the dismissal of a judge who had become unfit for work due to long-term illness. The Court granted the application.[7] Another case submitted to the Procurator General

---

[7] Dutch Supreme Court, 12 July 2013.

concerned a judge who had been involved in a criminal investigation. He had been accused of stalking. It was a private matter: the judge had a disagreement with other family members regarding the care of an elderly relative. The Public Prosecution Service decided to defer prosecution, on certain conditions. After consulting the Procurator General, the president of the court gave the judge a written reprimand for compromising the dignity of his office. This is a disciplinary measure provided for by the law.

A third case notified to the Procurator General also concerned a judge who had become involved in a criminal investigation, this time into a traffic accident. The judge's car had been in a collision with a scooter at a junction with a cycle path where visibility was poor. The scooter rider suffered injuries. A criminal investigation into the judge's actions followed. The district court acquitted her on the principal charge of causing an accident through negligence, resulting in serious bodily injury. It did find it proven however that by failing to give way to the scooter she had caused a dangerous situation on the road under section 5 of the Road Traffic Act 1994. The court ordered her to pay a €500 fine and imposed a suspended disqualification from driving with an operational period of three months. Under the law, a judge can be dismissed if he is convicted of a serious offence. Causing a dangerous situation on the road is a minor offence; in this case there were therefore no grounds for dismissal. Nor did the Procurator General see any grounds for a disciplinary measure.

The decisions made by a judge may reveal that he lacks the requisite legal knowledge, for instance if he consistently applies old legislation because he hasn't kept his professional expertise up-to-date. But even then, it is not the decisions that determine what happens. Only the lack of the necessary skills and knowledge, as evidenced by his decisions and amounting to acting in a way irreconcilable with judicial office, can provide grounds for dismissal. Incidentally, dismissal is not automatic if a judge is not functioning properly. Like any other public servant, judicial officers can only be dismissed as unfit for office if they first have been informed in a timely manner of their shortcomings and enabled to improve their performance. Where necessary, supervision and guidance must be offered.

IX. COMPLAINING ABOUT JUDGES

Do judges suffer from 'Monday blues'? It is quite possible. Do they always treat everyone properly? Maybe not always. Is this permissible?

No it isn't. Privilege entails responsibility. Which is why there must be a way of complaining about a judge's conduct, as distinct from the decisions courts arrive at. For the latter, there is the system of legal remedies.

A complaints procedure is a good thing because judges are not infallible. They may act incorrectly in their dealings with parties, witnesses, victims, lawyers and experts. And a successful complaint must lead to a sanction. The UK has set up a complaints system. The Judicial Conduct and Investigations Office (JCIO) plays a role in this. The Netherlands also has a complaints system. Here, the courts themselves are involved.

8

Cherish the Rule of Law!

A NUMBER OF Western European countries rank extremely high in the World Justice Project's Rule of Law Index I mentioned in Chapter 1. In 2016 Denmark topped the list, followed by Norway, Finland, Sweden, the Netherlands, Germany, Austria, New Zealand, Singapore and the UK. The Index investigates over a hundred countries every year on the basis of indicators including constraints on government powers, order and security, respect for human rights and the quality of the administration of justice. Safeguarding the rule of law is our shared responsibility. Even in economically difficult times we must ensure that we pass it on intact to the next generation. From a global perspective, what we have here in Europe is a fantastic achievement we can be very proud of. But that is no reason to become complacent. In this book, I have made a number of suggestions for improvement; many others are possible. Judges will have to remain alert and open to change. Fortunately, an open attitude has become increasingly the norm in recent years.

I would add that I am proud of judges in countries like the UK and the Netherlands who perform so outstandingly. And being a judge is a very rewarding profession: society confers on them an important task that they must fulfil impartially and independently. I consider it a great privilege to have been able to perform that task. And I believe we must make the reasons for the rule of law clear. People must become aware of its significance for the freedom of every single individual. It is not just the plaything of lawyers. Academics and politicians who are not lawyers sometimes neglect this duty. It is essential that our political and social leaders remain clear on this issue: the rule of law is vital to every one of us. We want to have equal opportunities, we want an executive and a judiciary that operate independently from each other, we want fundamental rights to be respected and we want everyone to have unimpeded access to an independent and impartial tribunal. It is the responsibility of all those who are leaders in society, be they politicians or social leaders, business people, those responsible for the education of youngsters, or (and in particular) the legal profession and the judiciary to remedy the lack of understanding of the immense importance of the rule of law by constantly emphasising it. Ensuring that everyone has equal opportunities is indeed a major challenge, certainly in countries where minority groups face significant problems. What is needed in such cases is an open and honest debate between majority and minority groups. It helps to explain the meaning of the rule of law, the role of judges, what they do in practice and why this is so valuable. Because the more familiar people are with these issues, the more they will appreciate their importance. All students, not only law students, have to be confronted with the significance of the rule of law. In fact this should be taught in secondary schools. Aharon Barak compared the rule of law with a tree: 'Trees that we have nurtured for many years may be uprooted with one stroke of the axe'.[1]

I would like to conclude with a line from a song by Dutch singer Huub van der Lubbe which sums up the underlying message of this book: 'You'll only know what you're missing when she's gone'.

---

[1] Aharon Barak, *The judge in a democracy*, Princeton University Press 2006, p 22.

Index

124   *Index*